Best wishes from the author.
Michael Berry

WITHDRAWN
FROM STOCK

# CORK AIRPORT

# AN AVIATION HISTORY

by

MICHAEL BARRY

**AER RIANTA**

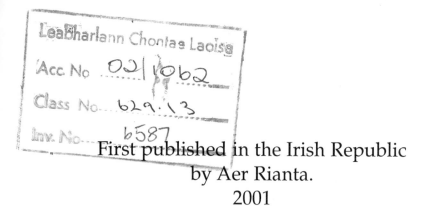
First published in the Irish Republic
by Aer Rianta.
2001

Copyright © Michael Barry (2001)

ISBN  0 9540591

Front Cover  Photographs – Gabriel Desmond

Printed and bound by Litho Press, Midleton, Co. Cork.

Joe O'Connor, General Manager Cork Airport

# Other books by Michael Barry.

**No Flowers By Request** - Short Stories (1979).

**Poems For Your Pleasure** (1980).

**An Affair of Honour** - Irish Duels and Duelists (1981).

**The Romance of Sarah Curran** (1985).

**The Story of Cork Airport** (1988).

**International Aviation Quiz Book** Vol. I (1989).

**By Pen and Pulpit** -The Life and Times of
Priest-Author Canon Patrick Sheehan (1990).

**The Mystery of Robert Emmet's Grave** (1991).

**International Aviation Quiz Book** Vol. II (1991).

**Great Aviation Stories** Vol. 1 (1993).

**Fermoy GAA Club History** 1886-1995  (1996).

**Great Aviation Stories** Vol. II (1997).

**On Wings Of Song**  - Fermoy Choral Society
Through The Years (1999).

# FORMER CORK AIRPORT MANAGERS

Vincent Fanning
Oct. 1961- Feb. 1967

Paddy O'Grady
May 1967 - Sept.1973

Gerry Holohan
Sept. 1973 – March 1984

Barry Roche
March 1984-March 1998

*This book is dedicated to all those whose efforts enabled Cork Airport to become a reality and to all who have worked there during the past forty years and contributed to its success.*

# FOREWORD

I had the privilege of working with the author at Cork Airport since 1966 until his retirement in 1987. One thing is certain - this book will contain nothing that fails a test of integrity. His previous publication about Cork Airport proved to be a very valuable reference book and I know that this version, which celebrates the airport's 40th anniversary, will be widely used for research and planning and many other purposes. It is also, of course, a nostalgic book for many in the aviation community as well as for those who have used Cork Airport over the years. May it revive fond memories for many readers; may it be a tribute to the many fine people who have served in and travelled through Cork Airport over the decades; and may it be a source of knowledge and inspiration for those who will carry the torch in the future. On behalf of Aer Rianta I thank Michael Barry for this invaluable contribution to aviation history.

Joe O'Connor, Cork Airport General Manager

# INTRODUCTION

When I wrote *The Story of Cork Airport* in 1988, I never envisaged that thirteen years later I would write another book on the same subject. Yet, in that brief time span, development, expansion and modernisation have taken place to such an extent that the airport is barely recognisable from that which existed in 1988.

Today's Cork Airport is a very much enlarged and thoroughly modern complex, with state of the art technology that places it on a par with any comparable sized airport in the world, fully equipped to take its place in the new millennium. At the end of the airport's first full year of operation in 1962, the passenger figure was 76,184; in 1988 that figure had risen to 541,524. By the end of the year 2000, the figure had more than trebled the '88 figure to 1,680,160. A new modern Hotel and Business Park have given the airport an added dimension and a modernisation programme over the next five years costing £61m is well under way.

In this book, which commemorates the 40th anniversary of Cork Airport, I have endeavoured to capture by word and in picture the aviation spirit of the people of Cork, not just over the past forty years but over a period of seventy three years, the first thirty three of those years being of tireless effort and dedication, spent in pursuing the ultimate goal of getting an airport for Cork.

Cork Harbour Commissioners were the first of those early pioneers. Among those who followed were Richard F. O'Connor, Cork Co. Surveyor and transport visionary; Cork Corporation; Cork Co. Council; the Cork Aero Club and above all, Cork Airways Co. formed by George Heffernan and Dan Cullinane, both Corkmen who gave the city its first commercial airport at Farmers Cross in 1948.

The book is a tribute, not alone to those who have served at Cork Airport over the years, but also to those early pioneers who, by their foresight and perseverance, paved the way in ensuring that Cork should take its rightful place in the world of civil aviation.

Michael Barry

# References.

Some of the references used in the writing of this book were originally those used by me in The Story of Cork Airport (1988).

Survey - Chamier, Gilbert Lodge & Co. London (1936); Runways & Associated Works at Cork Airport - T. L. Hogan & B. Clancy; Irish Parliamentary Debates; The First Twenty Years – P. J. Crean; Cork Airways Files – Courtesy D. Cullinane; Cork Harbour Commissioners Archives; Cork Co. Library (Ref. Section); Irish Examiner, Evening Echo, Irish Independent and Irish Times Newspapers; A Study of Disruption to Operations at Cork Airport due to Adverse Weather Conditions – P. Bracken; The Flight of the Iolar – Brendan Share; Cork Corporation Files – Cork Archives Institute; Review of Irish & UK Files on the loss of the Aer Lingus Viscount St. Phelim on 24th March 1968 – Air Accident Investigation Unit, Dept. of Public Enterprise; Tragedy at Tuskar Rock – Dermot Walsh; Runway Magazines – Aer Rianta; Aer Rianta Press Office; Aer Rianta Technical Services Dublin; Press Cutting Files - Aer Rianta Cork Airport; Guinness Ireland Archives; Cork Airport and its Aircraft – G. Desmond, G. Farrar. G., N, & P. Frost and R. Shanahan.

# ACKNOWLEDGEMENTS

The author wishes to acknowledge Aer Rianta's contribution to the research and preparation of this book.

My very sincere thanks to Joe O'Connor, General Manager Cork Airport, Sheila Murphy, Asst, Gen. Manager, John Smyth, Marketing Manager and Lilibeth Horne, Commercial Manager, for their assistance, encouragement and co-operation.

Without the outstanding assistance and infinite patience of Denis Maher, Duty Manager, Cork Airport this book could not have been written. His support went far beyond the call of duty. To him I owe a deep debt of gratitude.

I gratefully acknowledge the generosity of the Irish Examiner in providing many photographs, especially those of the early aviation years in Cork including Cobham's Air Circus at Ballincollig (1933), the opening of Farmers Cross Airfield (1948) and the opening of the present Cork Airport at Ballygarvan (1961). In this regard, I greatly appreciate the co-operation and assistance given by Paddy Barker, Asst. Image Editor together with Pat Good and Lilian Caverly of the Photographic Dept.

My grateful thanks to Gabriel Desmond for his excellent help and advice and of course for his numerous historical aviation photographs used throughout the book and on the book cover.

Many thanks to the following for supplying data on a variety of matters: Noel Bradley (Aer Lingus AFC); Dan Scanlan (Aer Lingus Golf); Dan Callanan (Cork Airport Golfing Society); Billy McCarthy (Cork Airport Angling Club); Donie Harris (Cork Airport GAA Club); Comdt. Kevin Byrne (Irish

Air Corps); Lt. Cdr. P.C. Richings RN (The Royal Naval Air Search and Rescue Service); John Harrington (Airport Business Park); Michael Beasley (Airport Car Parks); Sean McAdam O'Connell and Martin Ryan (Irish Aviation Authority); Bernie Howard, (Brymon Airways); Michael Healy C.A.S.O. (Airport Police & Fire Service); Gerry O'Donnell (Aviation Fuel); Jon Field, Airports Div. Dept. of Enterprise (Ministers & Ministers of State in Dept. of T.& P. since 1961); Gerry Holohan (Memoir); Brian Cox (Aer Lingus); Donal Crowley (Customs & Excise); Barbara Kiernan, (Ryanair); Claire Vaughan (British Airways); Malcolm Coupar (CityFlyer Express); Bill Daly (Engineering Maintenance); John Smyth (Marketing); Lilibeth Horne (Commercial); Peter O'Connell (CHC Ireland Helicopters); Alan Long (Servisair); Brian Doyle (Met Eireann); Catherine Cronin (Great Southern Hotels), Thomas Cullen (Kylemore Catering). My sincere thanks also to Tim Cadogan, Cork Co. Library, Brian McGee, Cork Archives Inst. for data supplied. and to The Royal Canadian Mounted Police, for verifying my script on the investigations to date into the Air India Disaster of 1985.

To the many who took time to talk to me, those who sent me press cuttings and private photographs and to the many airport staff, present and past, who co-operated in my research, I am deeply grateful. Special mention of the following is made :- Ray Shanahan, Geoffrey Farrar, Johnny Buckley, Tim Bradley, John Collins, Brendan Clancy, B.E., Jack McGrath, B.E., Barry Roche, Gerry Holohan, Gerry Fanning, Ian Howley, Michael Murtagh, Noreen Lynch, Bried Walsh, Gerry Tracey, Tim Murphy, Tom Fitzgerald, Donie Harris, Cait Ward and Yvonne Whitley.

I greatly appreciate the time spent by Máirín Ahern, Tom Fitzgerald, Tom O'Driscoll and Gabriel Desmond reading the manuscript.

# CONTENTS

# 1

## CHAPTER ONE

From that memorable day in December 1903 when the Wright brothers made the first heavier than air flight, aviation made rapid strides. When the First World War began a little more than a decade later, military aircraft played a large role in the conflict. Even before the war, private flying was taken up in many countries and Ireland was no exception. Lord Carbery made several flights from the Mardyke in Cork. On board one of them was Miss L. E. Townsend of Lislenane, Clonakilty, who was credited with being the first lady passenger in a flying exhibition in Ireland. Lord Carbery later became a very prominent aviator.

Following the end of the war in 1918, very many military aviators were demobilised and several continued their flying careers in civil aviation. In mid-June 1919, two British flyers, Capt. John Alcock and Lieut. Arthur Brown made the first non-stop trans-Atlantic air crossing when they flew from Newfoundland and landed in Clifden, Co. Galway. Progress in civil aviation development was slow at first; however, by the end of the 1920s great advances had been made in many parts of the world. In Ireland however, following the formation of the State, there came the Civil War and later the Economic War. Against that background, civil aviation took a rear seat. In Cork, there were many outside politics anxious

Lord Carbery (left) with his mechanic at the Mardyke, Cork in 1914.
*Photo – Courtesy Irish Examiner*

that the city be linked by air as soon as possible, not alone with Dublin and other Irish cities but also with the United Kingdom and the Continent of Europe.

Aviation really came to the fore in the minds of people when, in May 1927, Charles Lindbergh wrote himself into the annals of aviation history by making the first solo flight across the Atlantic in his plane The Spirit of St. Louis. On the 11th April 1928, Irishman Major James Fitzmaurice, with Gunther Von Hunefeld and Captain Herman Köhl made the first east west crossing of the Atlantic in a Junkers W33 aeroplane called The Bremen.

As interest in aviation increased, the people of Cork and its surrounds became more aware of its potential. Cork Harbour Commissioners were among the first public bodies in the city to realise the benefits that would accrue from an air base. On 27th September 1928 they invited Colonel Charles Russell, a former officer commanding the Irish Army Air Corps, to address them. Afterwards, the Cork Harbour Engineer was directed to prepare "a full report on the suitability or otherwise of the Port of Cork for the landing and taking off of aeroplanes or sea planes." It was the first move in what was to be a long series of surveys, reports, set backs and delays before Cork eventually got its airport.

The Harbour Commissioners were also very anxious that a Government policy statement be made on the whole question of the development of commercial aviation in the Irish Free State. Meanwhile, a motion was carried at their meeting requesting them to undertake an aerial survey of the port of Cork and its environs.

The Government did look into the feasibility of an air service that would be operated nationally. The report pointed out that a considerable amount of money would have to be spent in setting up such a service and that the State would have a commitment in providing some of that money in the formative years. Successive Governments were slow in getting involved in airport projects, due to the costs involved but were also very opposed to allowing a fully licensed airport to be built by private enterprise and operating scheduled services. Cork was the main victim of this policy.

The Harbour Commissioners wrote to famous British aviator, Sir Alan Cobham, requesting him to look at the facilities available for aviation in the port of Cork, when he visited the city. He addressed them on 31st January 1929 saying that Cork was really ahead in its willingness to consider the question of an airport. The ideal situation would be an aerodrome and seaplane base combined, as close to the city as possible. He added that Cork was in a unique position as an airport location for services to England, the Continent and eventually to America. Ironically, the advent of trans-Atlantic aviation and its rapid development sounded the death knell for the liner trade, leaving once bustling ports such as Cobh deserted.

The Commissioners were very positive in their approaches to develop Cork Harbour as a seaplane base but did not get great encouragement from the State. As the 1930s began to unfold, the trans-Atlantic seaplane was becoming a reality and would open up great possibilities for Cork Harbour through air links with the United States and Canada, should a base be available.

At the beginning of September 1932 at the Ottawa Imperial Conference, agreement was reached between the Irish Free State, Great Britain and Canada to explore the possibility of cutting twelve hours from the three days twenty two hours it took for mails between London and Montreal.

To achieve this, it was felt that Cork would become an important base. On arrival by liner at Cobh, the mails would be rushed by air to London. When the press carried the story, hopes were raised but Cork was not to benefit.

The dawn of 1933 brought an airport no nearer to Cork. However, Richard F. O'Connor, Cork County Surveyor, had also been keeping a close eye on aviation developments. A man of great vision, he had a deep interest in all things pertaining to Cork City and its surrounds, especially in the field of transport. He presented his ideas to a group of interested Cork people on 4th July 1933.

The Chairman of Imperial Airways, Sir Eric Geddes had stated a short time previously that the crossing of the Atlantic by seaplanes would be an accomplished fact within five years. Two terminal ports had already been considered, one at Botwood, Newfoundland and the other at Southampton in the UK. It was felt that there should be an intermediate base in Ireland. Because of that, Mr. O'Connor thought it imperative that a Cork airport be set up at once. This would enable it to take advantage of the existing liner traffic and establish air routes before a seaplane crossing of the Atlantic became a reality. The first object of the scheme, he said, was to gain control of English and Continental transatlantic mail services. A proportion of passenger and light goods traffic would in the ordinary course follow the mail routes.

The proposed aerodrome site was at Belvelly, an area between Great Island, Little Island and the mainland. It would necessitate the reclamation of about 460 acres of tidal mudflats. For seaplane landings, the large stretch of water situated east of a line drawn from Cuskinny to Corkbeg, was thought to be the most suitable. His ideas for an air base attracted the attention of Flight, a very reputable British avi-

5

Sir Alan Cobham pioneer of the Air Circus in the UK and Ireland

ation journal. It was a great boost for Richard F. O'Connor's plans but again the Government showed little interest.

In 1933, While O'Connor was putting forward his plans for an airport, aviation was being publicised throughout Ireland by Sir Alan Cobham and his famous air circus. He began Aviation Day in England to make the British people more air conscious. He toured the UK with his team of aviators and as a result, many looked back with pride and said that it was due to him that they got their first experience of flying. From those beginnings, there developed the famous air circus team of daredevil flyers who, for four years, continued to give aerobatics displays that made spectators gasp in wonder. It was estimated that between three and four million saw those air displays.

In an effort to make Irish people more aviation conscious, he sought the approval of the Department of Industry and Commerce to stage an air display at eight centres in the Irish Free State - Dublin, Cork, Waterford, Clonmel, Limerick, Galway, Bundoran and Dundalk. The Cork site at Ballincollig had been part of a British garrison complex.

Cobham's Air Circus came to Cork on Wednesday and Thursday 5th and 6th July 1933. It consisted of 12 machines – Gypsy Moths, Tiger Moths, Fox Moths, Handley Page aircraft and an Auto Giro. They certainly made the people of Cork look skyward as they swooped low over the city advertising their arrival. The country was sweltering under a heat wave as thousands made their way to Ballincollig. One small plane caught their fancy as it put on an aerobatic display. The two day air circus was a resounding success and created both an awareness and an interest in aviation that otherwise wouldn't have been possible. It highlighted too the necessity of an airport for Cork. Sir Alan Cobham later inspected

A busy airfield scene at Cobham's Air Circus at Ballincollig. in July 1933.
*Photo – Courtesy Irish Examiner*

the site at Belvelly and was greatly impressed. He said "I look upon it as a magnificent aeroplane and seaplane base. It is one of the best sites I have seen in Ireland."

Because of the great interest in aviation, which was developing in the southern capital, City Manager Philip Monahan and members of the Corporation were anxious that Ballincollig should be made into a temporary municipal aerodrome, pending construction of a permanent air base for Cork. However, the Government wouldn't agree to it.

A branch of the Irish Aero Club was formed in Cork in April 1934 and for a short time following the formation of the Club, the members did their flying at Fermoy Aerodrome. In July of that year, Messrs J. W and J. T. Young placed a site at Farmers Cross, close to where Cork Airport is now situated, at the disposal of the Aero Club. As well as having a large flying membership, the Club played a strong role in trying to get Cork an airport.

Despite the intense activity of public bodies and representatives in the Cork area in presenting a case for an airport, it would appear that even by then, Cork Harbour as a seaplane base was out of the running. An article had appeared in Flight magazine for 2nd November 1933, which stated "Colonel and Mrs. Lindbergh left Southampton on October 23 for Ireland arriving in Galway the same day after having circled over Cork harbour. He (Lindbergh) is continuing his survey flight in search of a possible route for a transatlantic airway". The famous aviator had been retained from 1931 all through the 1930s as a consultant on the establishment of transatlantic bases. How well that was understood at that time by those involved in the aviation scene in Cork is not very clear.

Coming in to land at Cobham's Air Circus Ballincollig 1933.
*Photo – Courtesy Irish Examiner*

At the beginning of December 1935, the first steps involving the Free State in transatlantic air services were taken at a conference in Ottawa where Irish, United Kingdom, Canadian and Newfoundland government officials met. Among the matters discussed and agreed was the establishment of an airmail service, which would, at a later stage, include a passenger and freight service. Eventually it was decided that Foynes should be the seaplane base and Rineanna later to be called Shannon Airport for landplanes. Seaplanes did not make the impact that was first expected and as the war years progressed, the development of the land plane outstripped them. Foynes operated as a seaplane base for some years but it was abandoned in 1945 following the end of World War 11 and Shannon Airport, was built. The era of the commercial seaplanes to Ireland was over.

Since its inception, Cork Aero Club had financial problems and its position became more acute during the early years of the war. Despite efforts to keep the club functioning, it was obliged to cease activities in 1942. However, mindful of the role it had played in aviation, the Club, before its closure, issued a statement as follows:

The Cork Aero Club views with the gravest concern the fact that no work has yet been undertaken to provide Cork with a major airport. As regards the future, they consider that a city and port such as Cork, without an airport, will in the post war world be in much the same position as a town without a railway station fifty years ago.

By the middle of the 1930s, developments in aviation were moving rapidly and locations, once thought as ideal for an airport, were now being looked at less favourably than heretofore. A further in-depth survey of likely sites in the Cork area was needed and was undertaken by a British firm,

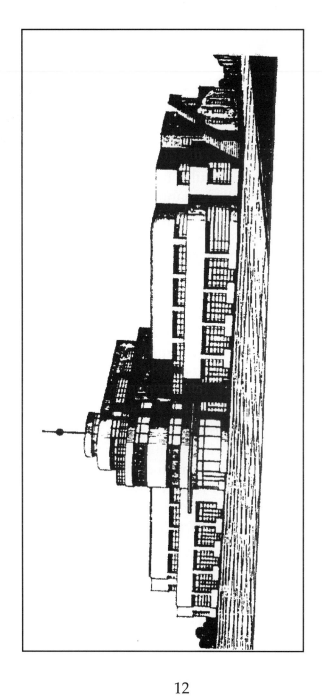

An artist's impression of the proposed Cork Airport at Ahanesk, Midleton 1936.

Messrs. Chamier, Gilbert-Lodge & Co. They published their report in August 1936.

Of the very many sites, old and new they examined, the only site found satisfactory was that at Ahanesk Midleton between Knockgriffin and Belvedere. The report stated:

"We are satisfied that at Midleton, an airport can be constructed which within six months could secure a Class 'A' Certificate and which is capable of extension. We are quite satisfied that, on this site, Cork has an airport adequate for both present and as far as can be foreseen, future requirements in suitable surroundings and within easy reach of the city. We believe this to be the only site on which a practicable and entirely satisfactory aerodrome could be made at modern expenditure and within a reasonable period of time."

The Government approved a proposal to establish a land airport for Cork in 1939. Of the initial cost, they would pay 45% and the balance would be met from Local Authority funding. It was expected that the airport would be built on the Midleton site.

The outbreak of World War II in September 1939 caused all those plans to be abandoned. As the war dragged on, the increased participation by aircraft in the conflict highlighted the great advances that had been made in aviation in the course of a few years. This created a new dimension with regard to airport sites, their location and their suitability.

Up to the time that Cork Airport was eventually built, successive Governments were accused of dragging their feet regarding the airport project. There is a certain amount of justification for these accusations, but on the other hand it is to their credit for having deliberated very carefully, especially after the war, before making a final decision, despite the enormous pressures they were under.

Richard F. O'Connor died in 1940, his great ambition, an airport for Cork, unrealised. There was no likelihood of any major move being made towards building an airport for Cork, at least until hostilities had ceased. Because of the rapid developments and advances being made in aviation, the Government felt it prudent to have further surveys of potential airport sites carried out. They were undertaken by the Office of Public Works on three sites in 1943 to discover a suitable airport location near Cork City.

The survey results were narrowed down to two locations - the site at Ahanesk, near Midleton and that at Ballygarvan, five miles south of Cork.

Both the Ballygarvan and Midleton sites were compared under the headings of cost, approaches, meteorological conditions, runway grades and convenience of location. With regard to cost, it was felt unnecessary to take into account items such as land acquisition and enclosure, buildings, aprons, concrete runways, lighting etc., which would be about the same on either site. This also applied to the cost of drainage. The cost of the full development at Ballygarvan was estimated at around £100,000 for grading, levelling and grass runways only. Similar work at Midleton would have been £14,000 less.

With regard to the approaches, Ballygarvan was found to be superior to Midleton. The degree and importance of the superiority of Ballygarvan in this respect was felt to be a matter on which aeronautical opinion should be obtained. The survey proposed not to express any opinion on the relative merits of the two locations from a meteorological point of view because specialised expert advice was needed. It was considered that the runway grades obtainable at Ballygarvan were definitely better than those at Midleton and finally, since Ballygarvan was only 5 miles from Cork city and Ahanesk 12 miles, the former was superior from the point of view of location. Summing up the survey findings, the Airport Engineer-in-Charge from the Board of Works recommended that, subject to expert advice on meteorological conditions etc., that the Ballygarvan site be chosen. The survey was submitted to the Airport Construction Committee of the Department of Industry & Commerce on 6th August 1943 and was adopted. The Committee affirmed that, excluding the meteorological conditions, the advantages of the Ballygarvan site outweighed Midleton.

With this information to go on, the Airport Construction Committee recommended that weather observation stations be set up as soon as possible at both Ballygarvan and Ahanesk to gather information over a period that would include the winter months. Nothing, however, was done until the war was over. Meanwhile, a further inspection of likely aerodrome sites was carried out by the Board of Works early in 1944 but Ballygarvan still remained the choice, subject to meteorological reports.

The Meteorological Service set up temporary observing stations at both locations on 16th September 1946. Michael (Mickey)) Murtagh was in charge of the Ballygarvan station and Ahanesk was under the supervision of John Doherty. Both officers had been transferred from Shannon. The winter of 1946/47 was one of the severest for many years and the observations for Ballygarvan were made in an area of Lehenaghmore, which was part of Cottrell's farm. Cottrell's house stood in its own grounds and had its entrance and driveway close to where the main entrance to the airport now is. The farm-house was situated about four hundred yards from the road. Cottrells were large farmers who, at

A German seaplane at Cobh shortly before World War II. The magnificent Cobh Cathedral is in the background.

*Photo – Courtesy Irish Examiner*

16

that time, supplied milk to the south side of the city. Observing the weather was recalled vividly by Mickey Murtagh.

"Working conditions then for myself and a staff of four, Ray O'Loughlin, Marty Brennan, Connie Beare and Tom Kelly were very rough. We had an office, if you could call it that in one of the out buildings of the farmyard – a loft with stone steps going up from outside. There was no electricity, just an oil lamp and oil heater. Things were very primitive. There was no telephone and the daily observations were sent by post to Dublin. In order to carry out the observations, staff had to walk from the 'office' across fields often deep in snow to where the instrumentation site was, and this had to be done every hour of the day and night. It was a winter of very heavy snow falls and the avenue to Cottrell's house was piled high on either side with snow."

Meteorological observations for the six months period October 1946 to the end of March 1947 at both Ahanesk and Ballygarvan were the subject of a meteorologist report early in May 1947. The report gave Midleton the advantage. Of course the winter of 1946/47 had been one of the worst for many years. The May report of 1947, however, pointed out that a series of observations covering a much longer period than six months would be necessary to really determine the relative suitability of different sites from a meteorological point of view. Observations continued at Ballygarvan for a further three months.

Meanwhile, the building of Dublin Airport commenced in 1937 and the first passenger service flight was on 19th January 1940. The end of World War II saw the opening of Shannon Airport. Cork was the poor relation and was to remain so for many years.

Liam Cosgrave, T.D., Parliamentary Secretary to an Taoiseach, seen here addressing the large crowd, when he officially opened Farmers Cross Airfield on Sunday 9th May 1948.

*Photo – Courtesy Irish Examiner.*

The people of Cork were weary from hearing of the many plans and surveys being carried out. In a sense of desperation in 1947, two prominent Cork business men, George Heffernan and Dan Cullinane came together and decided that, as the authorities were not going to provide Cork with an airport in the foreseeable future, they themselves would do so by private enterprise.

. It was decided to establish an airfield at Farmers Cross where the Cork Aero Club did their flying. A company was formed called Cork Airways Company in which both Heffernan and Cullinane had an equal share. The Company's secretary was Jean Davies, who was attached to Heffernan's Shipping Agency. A lease of the land was obtained for 25 years and an aerodrome licence was sought early in 1948. Before it could be granted, the Dept. of Industry and Commerce laid down stipulations, one of which was the removal of a plantation of trees dividing two fields. Some trees had also to be removed along the southeast boundary.

Work was carried out very promptly, two fields were made into one and the ground was leveled. Only one grass runway was available measuring 860x260 yards at its widest running almost east west. A cross-runway running almost north south could be made to a length of about a mile, should business necessitate such development. When the required work was carried out, a licence was granted for the field on a restricted basis. Private and charter flights could operate but not scheduled services. There were certain restrictions as to how and when the charters would operate such as in daylight hours only, etc. Cork Airways Company was seeking much more than that but at least it was a start.

At the opening of Farmers Cross Airfield 9th May 1948.

L: to R:- George Heffernan, Director Cork Airways Co; Lt. Col. W. J. Keane, James Hickey T.D.,E. Gayer, Gen. Manager Cork Harbour Commissioners, Liam Cosgrave,T.D., Parliamentary Sec. to An Taoiseach, who officially opened the airfield; Michael Sheehan, T.D. Lord Mayor of Cork, Dan Cullinane, Director Cork Airways, Sen. Richard Anthony, E. O'Neill, W. Cullinane. P. D. Lehane, T.D.

*Photo – Courtesy Irish Examiner*

**Official Opening of Farmers Cross Airfield.**

Farmers Cross airfield was officially opened on the afternoon of Sunday 9th May 1948 by Liam Cosgrave, Parliamentary Secretary to An Taoiseach, in the presence of several thousand people, He praised the venture and pointed out the huge capital costs that the State had incurred regarding Dublin and Shannon airports. In his address he said: "I should certainly be very pleased to see private enterprise and private flying fields playing an important part in the development of civil aviation in this country." The speech was music to the ears of George Heffernan and Dan Cullinane but that music would be well out of tune in the years ahead.

The Company pressed ahead with private and charter flights as governed by its licence. In the charter area, a considerable amount of success was achieved and the marketing of the Airfield was done very efficiently. This, however, was totally inadequate to make it commercially viable and Cork Airways Company sought a licence to run scheduled air services. Cambrian Air Services, Cardiff, who had operated several charter flights to Cork had offered a daily service between the cities in April 1949. The Department of Industry and Commerce would not grant a scheduled air services licence on the grounds that the facilities available at the airfield were inadequate for scheduled operations because they did not include meteorological and radio services or sufficient approach, taxiway and runway lighting in instrument flying conditions.

So far as Cork Airways was concerned, it was the case of the chicken or the egg – which came first. The Company couldn't provide the necessary capital for the required facilities until business warranted it through scheduled services and those flights couldn't materialise without the required

Section of the crowd at Farmers Cross airfield on opening day 9th May 1948
*Photo - Courtesy Irish Examiner*

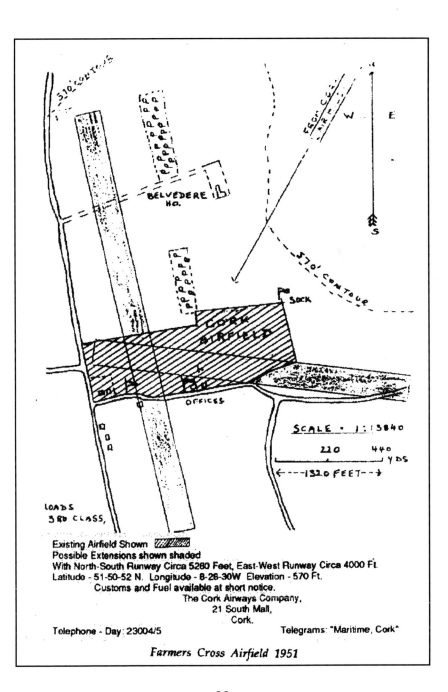

Existing Airfield Shown
Possible Extensions shown shaded
With North-South Runway Circa 5280 Feet, East-West Runway Circa 4000 Ft.
Latitude - 51-50-52 N. Longitude - 8-28-30W  Elevation - 570 Ft.
Customs and Fuel available at short notice.
The Cork Airways Company,
21 South Mall,
Cork.
Telephone - Day: 23004/5                    Telegrams: "Maritime, Cork"

*Farmers Cross Airfield 1951*

facilities. Meanwhile, a report came out, which the Government had sought from Aer Rianta, who at that time managed Dublin Airport. The main conclusions drawn, with regard to the commercial possibilities of air services to and from Cork, were that a Cork-London air service would be a fairly sound commercial proposition and that if Aer Lingus was to undertake regular services through Cork, night flying facilities would have to be provided in addition to the usual airport aids.

Many felt that the Government was paying lip service to Cork's requirements. It wasn't of course that straightforward. Apart from any arrangements entered into, the equipping of an airfield by the State to meet international standards was costly and finance was a scarce commodity in 1952. Also, in fairness, the site at Farmers Cross had never been chosen by the State as one suitable on which to build Cork's international airport. Mr. Lemass had stated in the Dail some time previously, that in relation to where Cork Airport should be located, he had set up an enquiry and he awaited the findings.

The Committee reported in July 1953 that, on balance, Ballygarvan was a better site than Midleton. On 6th January 1954, the Minister recommended to the Government that an airport for the operation of scheduled services to and from Cork city should be constructed at Ballygarvan and that it should have concrete runways. Midleton renewed its agitation without success. It was the end of the line too as far as scheduled services were concerned at Farmers Cross, although Cork Airways Company continued with their charter operations up to the time the new airport was opened.

Despite all the arguments put forward in its favour, Farmers Cross Airfield would never have been suitable for

Air Display at Farmers Cross 2nd September 1957
*Photo – Courtesy Irish Examiner*

development as an international airport worthy of the State's second city. However, there is no doubt but that Cork Airways Company pioneered what became a very long struggle following the end of World War II before Cork got its airport. More important still, it must never be forgotten that two private Cork citizens, George Heffernan and Dan Cullinane, put their own money into a project that provided the people of Cork and surrounding areas with an airport for twelve years when all they had been getting up to then were empty promises. Not one penny was made out of Farmers Cross airfield. In fact it always operated at a loss, which was borne by the generosity of the airfield's two directors.

In 1960, the year before the new airport was opened at Ballygarvan, Cork Airways Company wrote to the then Minister for Transport & Power, Mr. Erskine Childers seeking to recoup the losses they had suffered during the 12 years that Farmers Cross had been opened. It amounted approximately to £3900. That request was refused.

A party of Butchers from Jersey with Jean Davies, Sec. Cork Airways Co. (fourth from right) at Farmers Cross Airfield, August 1954.

*Photo –Courtesy Irish Examiner*

# 2

# CHAPTER TWO

In January 1957, the Government agreed in principle that an airport should be constructed at Ballygarvan. The site chosen was on the west side of the Cork-Kinsale road, about five miles from the city centre. It had an elevation of 480 feet above Ordnance Datum. The timetable of events was fixed eventually as follows - completion of plans February 1959; placing the contract May 1959; completion of the work May 1961.

The first major requirement for the new airport was land, sufficient not alone for runways, terminal building etc. but also to enable expansion and development take place in the future. To this end, the Department of Industry and Commerce decided to acquire close on 500 acres in the Ballygarvan area. This comprised two entire holdings, five part holdings and three County Council plots with cottages. One of the main holdings was that of Mrs. Winifred Cottrell containing just over 186 acres with house and outoffices in the townland of Lehenaghmore. Another was that of Thomas and Daniel Crowley with over 129 acres in the townland of Ballygarvan. The remaining land of concern to the project was 107 acres with house and outoffices belonging to Timothy Murphy of Ballygarvan; 5 acres belonging to William White of Lehenaghmore; 26 acres, the property of Matthew Mulcahy; 13 acres owned by Benjamin J. Hosford,

Gortangoulane, Ballygarvan and finally there were 3 Council cottages with plots of an acre each owned respectively by Matt Collins, Lehenaghmore, John Twomey, Ballygarvan and Daniel Horgan, also of Ballygarvan.

The acquiring of the land was a formidable undertaking but was carried out successfully in record time. In March 1958, Department Engineers, Pat Hackett, Edwin McCarthy and Brendan Clancy carried out a survey of the site. The latter became resident engineer at the airport on its completion. A labour force was recruited to assist in the work of cross-sectioning, trial hole digging, determination of obstacles in the approaches and water course investigations. After three months survey work, progress had fallen behind due to bad weather and two additional engineers were sent from Head Office to help complete the work.

Later, following the Government's approval of the proposal of the Minister of Transport and Power in July 1959 to invite tenders and place contracts for the construction of the airport at an estimated cost of one million pounds, the contract for the civil engineering works was given to Messrs John Paul & Co. Ltd., Dublin in October 1959. The completion date was set at 31st July 1961. The contract covered the levelling of the site and the construction of runways, apron and approach road.

On 5th November 1959 The Cork Examiner, which for many years championed the drive for an airport, carried a statement by Mr. Erskine Childers, Minister for Transport and Power, that the work on the one million pound airport would begin very soon and that construction of the runways and taxiways would proceed simultaneously with the airport buildings.

Beginning of Control Tower construction. Second from right is D.D. O'Leary, who joined Aer Rianta Maintenance when the airport opened and was Maintenance Operations Supervisor for many years until his death in 1998
*Photo – Courtesy Irish Examiner*

Laying the runways at Cork Airport 16th June 1960
*Photo – Courtesy Irish Examiner*

# We know where you're coming from. Look where we're going.

Cork Airport is an expanding gateway to Europe, attracting the best air carriers around. With over 40 airlines operating inwards and outbound you have easy access to a growing number of major UK and European destinations. And with the opening of the Lee Tunnel, Cork Airport is easier than ever to reach from

such counties as Waterford, Tipperary or Kilkenny. Now we want to reach even further and give you much more. For your comfort, convenience and safety we're investing £60m to include apron and terminal extensions, taxiways, airbridges, new cargo facilities multi-storey carparking and a new pier building. Come to Cork airport. We're going places.

*MOVING FORWARD FAST*

**AerRianta**
**CORK AIRPORT**

It was a major project. Several overhead electricity supply lines crossed the site and approaches, the principal one being the 38 KV line from Cork to Haulbowline. In all, about 10 miles of lines were removed by the ESB and re-erected clear of the airport. It was also necessary to remove close on 11 miles of banks, hedges and walls and 500 trees. On 7th March 1960, two gigantic earth-moving units moved on to the airport site. They were caterpillar 225 Turbo-charged Horsepower Rubber-tyred Scrapers, capable of carrying loads in excess of 20 tons at speeds of up to 30 mph. In order to obtain suitable grading for the runways etc, it was necessary to strip and replace about 17,000 cubic yards of topsoil and to excavate and place in-fill about 820,000 cubic yards of earth and rock. No imported filling was used except to form a base course for the concrete over part of the site. Rock excavation amounted to about 35,000 cubic yards but very little blasting was necessary. Weather conditions greatly affected progress with the excavation and filling work. Although the contract works began in November 1959, it wasn't possible to start filling until late April 1960. That work had to be suspended in October 1960 until the spring of 1961 because of the wet weather. The work was virtually completed during the summer of 1961.

Meanwhile, the work of laying the concrete runways, apron and approach road had begun in May 1960 and was completed in October 1961. In all, the area of concrete pavement laid down was 223,770 square yards – about 46 statute acres and the volume of concrete placed was 62,260 cubic yards.

Tenders were also sought for the erection of the plumbing plant for the airport water supply and for the structural steel work of the airport buildings, i.e. the Terminal, Control

Tower, Boiler House and Freight Building. The steel work contract was placed with Thomas Thompson, Ltd. Carlow and the buildings contract with John Jones, Ltd. Dublin. The Architect was L. M. Carroll, Chief Airports Architect of the Department of Transport and Power.

The electricity supply was taken at 10 KV from the overhead network. An underground cable went to the building area from the north west corner of the site and was continued to connect again with the overhead network on the east side of the site. Transformer capacity installed was 640 KVA and a diesel-powered automatic standby plant of 110 KVA capacity was provided to maintain the supply to essential services such as runway lighting, communications etc. in the event of mains failure. High intensity lights spaced 200 feet apart were provided along the runway edges and at the thresholds. All approaches were provided with approach lights of the standard centre line and cross-bar type.

As speculation grew about the progress being made on the building of the airport, airlines began to show an interest in operating services to and from it once it was opened. At a Cork Rotary Luncheon, Mr. P. J. Brennan, Secretary of Aer Lingus, estimated that Cork Airport would handle 30,000 passengers annually in its first few years of operation and it was expected that the figure would grow to 60,000 within five or six years. The figures quoted were on the conservative side and later exceeded all expectations. Mr. Brennan had earlier paid tribute to Cork Airways Company "for being so active in advocating the establishment of regular services to and from Cork and for doing so much to encourage public interest in the project."

It was announced by Mr. Erskine Childers on 19th May 1960 that Cork Airport would be managed by the

Department of Transport and Power. The completion date was given in the Dail as July 1961. As time went by, more airlines sought permission from both UK and Irish administrations to run services between the two countries. In early August 1960, Cambrian Airways, later to become the first UK company to service Cork Airport and continued to do so very effectively for many years, secured British Government approval for its proposed routes from London, Cardiff, Bristol and Swansea to Cork. Although it would be 12 months before the airport would become operational, Aer Lingus announced their fares from Cork. This followed a meeting of the representatives of 80 airlines who had agreed on 17th October 1960 at Cannes to reduce fares in several parts of the world. Aer Lingus quoted Cork-London (return) as £17.85 with an excursion fare of £15.30; Cork-Lourdes (return) £38.70 with an excursion fare of £30.45.

The construction of the airport continued to be hampered by bad weather. The rainfall was almost 70% above normal in the period July – October 1960. The Department of Transport & Power issued a statement to that effect and added

> "The Minister, however, expects to open the airport for restricted operations on 1st September 1961 subject to he being satisfied at that time that the restricted facilities likely to be available will enable operations to be conducted in accordance with international regulations. It is expected that the airport will be finally completed about the end of 1961."

Work began in mid-January 1961 by Cork Corporation and Cork Co. Council on improving the road from the city to the airport. The Corporation had control of the phase within the city boundary and the remainder was under the control of the Co. Council. The stretch of road involved was from Ballypehane to Lehenagh and thence to Farmers Cross. Forty-five men were employed initially but double that number was engaged when work was at its peak between April and August.

--- 

The airport was very much in the throes of construction when the first officer-in-charge of any of the services, Jack McGrath, B.E. arrived in January 1961. He was responsible for the installation of a vast network of communications and navigational aids, which included an Instrument Landing System (ILS), Marker Transmitters. Compass Locators and a Very High Frequency Omnidirectional Range (VOR). Also, at the south of the field was the main VHF receiver site. The erection of the buildings to house most of this equipment was part of the building contract. An exception was the VOR, which was of circular steel construction. Jack McGrath and staff from the Post Office Engineering Branch, Cork erected this. Cork. Simultaneously with the installation of the Communications and Navigational Aids, an Aeronautical Fixed Telecommunications network (AFTN) was set up. This was a teleprinter network which would link Aer Lingus, the Meteorological Service, Air Traffic Control and the Radio Service with the communication station at Ballygireen, Co. Clare and from there around the world. Most important of all was the sixteen channel recording system, the black box of the airport's communications.

--- 

April 1961 had the highest rainfall recorded by UCC since 1894 but work pressed ahead. Towards the end of the month, the appointment of the Cork Airport Manager was announced. He was John Vincent Fanning, then a 39 years old Assistant Principal Officer in the Aviation Section of the Department of Transport and Power. He had been educated at Christian Brothers Schools in Dublin and Cork. He entered the Civil Service in 1939 and served in the Department of Industry & Commerce before transferring to the Department of Transport & Power.

- - -

In May 1961, the ESB Contract Section began the installation of all runway and approach lighting, ancillary plant and providing power to all other services then being installed. In charge of the ESB contract was John Drennan from the Limerick ESB District. He later became head of the electrical staff at the airport in June 1962.

A severe jolt was given to the airport's construction contractors on the 30th April 1961 when 750 shift workers at the factories of Cement Ltd. at Limerick and Drogheda served strike notice for a reduced working week. The entire supply of cement for the airport construction was from Limerick. There was no immediate danger to the maintenance of progress on the site but each new day brought with it a reduction in cement stocks. The strike lasted until the end of the first week in June. Some delays in construction had inevitably been caused and the opening date was deferred to 16th October. The Department notified the airlines intending to operate services to and from Cork that "the 16th October 1961 had now been fixed as the date on which restricted operations may commence at the airport."

There was strong criticism of the delay, with particular reference to the Cork Film Festival, which was scheduled to run from 27th September to 4th October. A large number of tickets had already been sold in connection with the widely advertised package tour from Britain to the Festival. It was

Aer Lingus and Cambrian Airways on the ground at Cork Airport following their proving flights 12th October 1961.
*Photo –Courtesy Irish Examiner*

even suggested that daylight flights could be operated and a plea was made to politicians to impress on the Minister the urgency of the situation.

On the surface, the grounds for complaint were reasonable. There had been a four weeks cement strike during which time the airport contractors had some cement in stock. Now there was to be a seven weeks postponement before the airport could be opened. However, there were factors other than the cement strike causing the delays and if the Department of Transport and Power had been up front in disclosing them, they would have avoided a great deal of controversy.

The opening of the airport was not simply having concrete runways and a terminal building available. The prime concern at any airport is that of safety and international regulations on lighting, clearance of obstructions, availability of communications and navigational aids had to be met. The provision of Air Traffic Control, Meteorological and Radio Services, together with Fire and Rescue, had to be complied with, to meet the very high standards of the International Civil Aviation Organisation (ICAO), before a notice could officially be promulgated that the airport was operational. To have all those requirements on stream by a fixed date wasn't easy and the 16th October was certainly the earliest date that they could be met.

At the end of July '61, Aer Lingus announced the appointment of Cork man, Tadg Lynch, as their Station Superintendent for Cork Airport. He had joined Aer Lingus in 1946 and was based in Shannon. Another Corkonian, Gerry Holohan, was appointed assistant to the Airport Manager at the beginning of August. He had been an Executive Officer at Shannon in the Department of Transport & Power. Appointed as Officer-in-Charge of the

A group of Aer Lingus Loaders photographed on 12th Oct. 1961, when
Aer Lingus and Cambrian Airways carried out proving flights to Cork.
Top to Bottom:- Donie Ford, John O'Shea, Eddie Mullins, Mick Hayes
Jimmy Keane, Jim Forde, Eddie Hegarty.
*Photo – Courtesy Irish Examiner*

Meteorological Service at the new Airport was Michael (Mickey) Murtagh, who had initially carried out the weather survey at Ballygarvan in 1946.

Gerry Tracey was appointed Officer-in-Charge of the airport's Fire, Rescue and Security Service. A native of Limerick, he had previously served with the Auxiliary Fire Service during the Emergency (1939 -1945) and later with Limerick Fire and Ambulance Service. Appointed head of Air Traffic Control was Robert (Bob) Howley from Dublin Airport.

Meanwhile, as opening day for the airport drew near, Aer Lingus and Cambrian Airways announced in the press on 13th September 1961 "from October 16th, Cork is only minutes away from the main British cities."

Although the airport had not yet been officially opened, the first commercial plane, an Aer Lingus F27 Friendship EI-AKG named *St. Fiachra*, carried out a proving flight from Dublin on 12th October, designed to test the route and the landing facilities at the airport. It landed at 9.27 a.m. Capt. William J. Martin, a native of Cavan was in command and the co-pilot was Captain Joseph Steven Barrett from Youghal. On board the flight were many Aer Lingus officials and press. "We had a splendid flight" Captain Martin said "and we couldn't have been more fortunate with the day. It was a very pleasant surprise to see the airport and find it so good as it is. It is excellent from any point of view." The hostesses on the flight were the Company's Chief Hostess for Europe, Joan Doyle together with Joan Lee. Among those on board were Capt. J.C. Kelly Rogers, Aer Lingus Deputy Gen. Manager; Capt. W. J. Scott, Assistant General Manager (Technical) and Mr. G. H. Giltrop, Services Manager Aer Lingus.

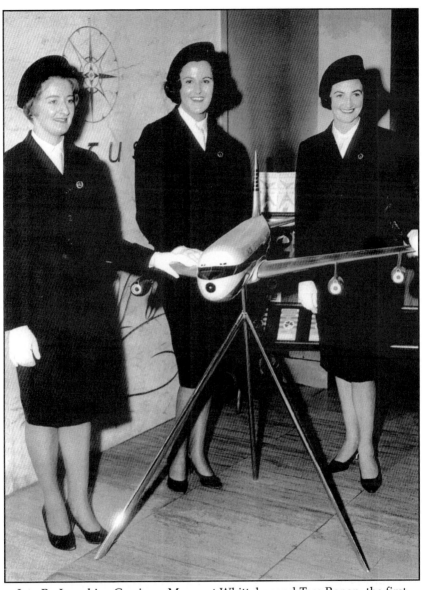

L to R:- Josephine Corrigan, Margaret Whittaker and Tess Ronan, the first
Aer Lingus ground hostesses at Cork Airport in October 1961.
*Photo – Courtesy Irish Examiner*

Cambrian Airways also carried out a proving flight that day in a Dakota DC-3 and so became the first overseas airline to land at Cork. The Commander of the flight was Chief Pilot G. Perrott and the Co-Pilot was Captain George Keeble. On board was Mr. Frank Clark, Personal Assistant to the Managing Director of the Company, Wing Commander L. B. Elwin, A.F.C.

The Airport opening hours were given in the press as follows:-

"To the end of October 1961, Mon. – Sat. (incl.), 0900-1830; Sunday 1230 -1800 and from Nov. 1961 to March 1962, Mon. – Sat. (incl.), 0900 -2000; Sunday – airport closed.

# OFFICIAL OPENING OF CORK AIRPORT

When Cork Airport opened for commercial flights on Monday 16th October 1961, it did so without any great publicity build up. There were no great crowds to witness the occasion and Irish Television was still a few months away. The day was overcast but unlikely to pose any flying problems. The airport was far from complete and it was a considerable time afterwards before the contractors made their departure. It is hard to visualise how it looked in contrast to today's modern structures and its many facilities. One must not forget the staff members on opening day and for a considerable time afterwards who worked under extremely difficult conditions. In many instances, the basic rudiments of office furniture had not yet replaced old packing cases. They were, however, pioneering times and it had been the case of all hands on deck to ensure that everything would be all right on the day.

Most Rev.Cornelius Lucey, Bishop of Cork blessing the airport on opening day.
*Photo – Courtesy Irish Examiner*

And so, under grey skies there was an air of great hope and expectations. Cork at last had got its airport after a wait of 33 years. Before the first aircraft landed, Bishop Cornelius Lucey conducted the ceremony of blessing the airport. He was accompanied by the Vicar General of the Diocese of Cork and Ross, Rev. Canon D. Murphy and by Rev. Canon Connolly, President of Farranferris College. The Airport Manager had met them on arrival. The Bishop also visited the terminal building and blessed the men who constructed it.

The first plane to arrive was an Aer Lingus Viscount from Dublin. On board were the Taoiseach, Seán Lemass and his wife, Jack Lynch, Minister for Industry and Commerce, Robert Briscoe, Lord Mayor of Dublin and senior officials of Aer Lingus and of Jacob & Co., the biscuit manufacturers. The Lord Mayor of Cork, Anthony Barry, with the Airport Manager, Vincent Fanning, welcomed the Taoiseach and his party.

In his address from the first floor balcony of the terminal building, Seán Lemass praised the new airport.

"This new airport in Cork summarises our purpose and helps us in our desire to have the world see us as a modern progressive State, coming rapidly and equally in line with all others in modern equipment and facilities."

Erskine Childers was also loud in his praise for the airport and for Cork in general.

"The word Cork has become synonymous with growth and efficiency and I have no doubt that the airport will prosper in the same way as other ventures, which have brought credit on their promoters and fame to the City and County of Cork."

An Taoiseach Sean Lemass T.D., Mrs. Lemass and Erskine Childers T.D Minister for Transport & Power, who arrived for the opening of Cork Airport, being escorted to the terminal by Anthony Barry T.D. Lord Mayor of Cork.

*Photo –Courtesy Irish Examiner*

Erskine Childers T.D., Minister for Transport and Power addressing the crowd from the first floor balcony on opening day.

*Photo – Courtesy Irish Examiner*

The Lord Mayor, in his address, said that Cork was now moving with great strides into the contemporary world. "We are facing a great period of expansion" he added "and the airport is an intrinsic adjunct to this progress."

There were six flights in and out of the airport on the first day. The much-discussed Cork-Dublin schedule service operated for the first time. This had raised some controversy when CIE had raised an objection to the fare set by Aer Lingus, which had, they claimed, competed unfairly with the rail fare. Following negotiations, the Minister directed the airline to set a fare, which would remove the competitive element of the service vis-à-vis the surface transport.

Cambrian Airways operated two flights on opening day, using DC-3s, then also called Dakotas. The first arrived at 12.50 pm carrying Cambrian senior officials and British press who were welcomed by the Airport Manager. The second DC-3 was their scheduled flight from London Heathrow, which landed at 6pm.

Jacobs Biscuits chartered a flight to Dublin for their 'Come Fly with Jacobs' promotion. Among their guests were famous sporting personalities including Cork hurler Christy Ring, Tony O'Reilly, international rugby player and Cork hurling trainer, Jim 'Tough' Barry. This was the first passenger-carrying plane to fly out of Cork.

Leading the official Irish party on the first scheduled flight to London was the Cork Lord Mayor. The Viscount aircraft 'St. Aodhan' had to hold over Heathrow for 42 minutes before landing due a backlog of flights resulting from heavy fog at London the previous day. Also, one of the runways was blocked for over an hour when an African plane burst three tyres on landing.

Among those about to make the first flight from Cork Airport to London on opening day seen here were Taoiseach Sean Lemass, T.D. and Mrs. Lemass, Jack Lynch,T.D. Minister for Industry & Commerce and Mrs. Lynch, Robert Briscoe, Lord Mayor of Dublin and Mrs. Briscoe together with Anthony Barry, Lord Mayor of Cork and Bishop Cornelius Lucey.

*Photo – Courtesy Irish Examiner*

There were no catering facilities at Cork Airport on opening day. In honour of the occasion, a lunch was held in the city by Cork Junior Chamber of Commerce, for the many aviation and civic dignitaries. That night, an Taoiseach, Sean Lemass, hosted a dinner at which he said:

"We are not seeking to join the European Community as any sort of poor relation, but as a developing country, which has studied all the implications of membership. ... Both as a symbol of our progress and of our purpose and as an important contribution to the already buoyant economy of Cork the coming into operational use of Cork Airport is a proper occasion for celebration and I am happy to be able to participate in it. ... When we embarked on the construction of this new airport, we knew we were investing in the future of Cork and that the investment would pay substantial dividends in economic progress and expanding employment opportunities."

In an article, in which he recalled opening day for the airport's 25th Anniversary Souvenir Programme, Gerry Holohan, Airport Manager (1973-1984), wrote:

"Those several weeks before October 16th were frantic as equipment and organisation was being readied. A score of technical and administration staff were transferred from Shannon and Dublin Airports – they spoke the 'Lingua' of airports – they spoke of ABLE BAKER CHARLIE and how EASY NAN FOXTROTS. They knew what role their particular Service played and how it dovetailed with the other Services. They gave confidence to the new hands – exciting times indeed. I would not have missed them.

'Come Fly with Jacobs' flight to Dublin on opening day.
*Photo – Courtesy Irish Examiner*

Monday October 16th was not the sunniest of days but it was mercifully free of any heavy threat of fog or mist. The newly laid highway from the city limits to the Airport gates looked splendid. The Airport Security personnel and local Gardai shared the stewarding of guests arriving by road. ... The tricolour flew proudly over Cork's new airport

There were no surging crowds at Cork Airport on opening day. The people of Cork took several days to realise that they had a modern wonder on their doorstep and the following Sunday they went to see it. Like a red-hatted crowd converging on Semple Stadium, they strained the resources of the Gardai and Airport Security staff. By midnight on the 16th, the speeches, receptions, lunches, dinners and more speeches were long over, the VIPs had been despatched by air to their destinations in Dublin, London, Cardiff and elsewhere. Staff on duty could not of course engage in any of the daylong city-based festivities; however, those duty bound minders on that day forged bonds and today, when over a pint their talk turns to October 16th 1961. Max Boyce's catch phrase is heard 'I was there Boy.' They have pride in a shared experience."

The Cork Examiner, later the Irish Examiner, which for years previously kept up the pressure on successive governments by numerous articles demanding an airport, recorded the opening day in picture and story. One Examiner journalist deserves special mention – the late Stephen Coughlan, forever synonymous with Cork Airport and with Farmers Cross airfield in earlier times.

At reception Imperial Hotel 16th Oct. 1961

L to R:-M. G. O'Mara, C.P.O. Customs & Excise; J.J. Kelly, Collector Customs & Excise; Gerry Holohan, Assistant to Airport Manager; P.J. Flanagan, Chief Air Traffic Control Officer; Bob Howley, OIC Air Traffic Control, Cork.

*Photo – Courtesy Irish Examiner*

# OICs on Opening Days

Vincent Fanning
Airport Manager

Brendan Clancy B.E
Airport Engineer

Tadgh Lynch
Station Manager, Aer Lingus

It is appropriate too to recall what the late Paddy Bracken, Air Traffic Conntrol Chief in Cork for many years, wrote in the 25th Anniversary Souvenir Programme a few months before his tragic death:

Staff members involved on opening day were imbued with a tremendous spirit, which overcame all difficulties. Although the full potential of the airport was not reached, nevertheless the traffic in the first year of operation greatly exceeded that predicted by the planners at the initial stages. The staff took pride and pleasure in the fact that the Southern Capital was at last linked by air to the important cities of England, Wales and the Continent of Europe. The dream had been realised, the pessimists were defeated; Cork Airport had come into being despite all the gloomy objections and in October 1961 became a reality.

The following were the first members of staff of the various services appointed to Cork Airport and who served there on opening day.

**Management and Engineering:-** Vincent Fanning, Gerry Holohan, Billy Barry, Mick Courtney, Nell Roche, Brendan Clancy, John O'Connell, Ger Kelleher, John Drennan, Billy O'Keeffe, D. D. O'Leary, Barry Cullinane, Jack Walsh, Brendan Lynch.

**Aer Lingus:-** Tadg Lynch, Joe Ward, Jimmy O'Regan, Tony Ryan, Morogh McHugh, Pat O'Connell, Barry Murphy, Tess Ronan, Jo Corrigan, Margaret Whittaker, Bob Lee, Charlie Dineen, Niall Sharkey, Donie Forde, Eddie Hegarty, Eddie Mullins, Jimmy Keane, Mick Hayes, Brendan Cannon (Major), Tom Foley, John O'Shea, Jim Forde (Congo), Paddy Greene.

**Air Traffic Control:-** Bob Howley, Paddy Bracken, Mick Mallon, Gerry Sammon, Tim Bradley, Austin Davis, Paddy

Jack McGrath B.E.
OIC Radio Service

Robert Howley
OIC Air Traffic Control

Michael Murtagh
OIC Met. Service

Herlihy, Tony Connolly, J. N. Crowe, Vincent Lane, Pat Doherty, Jimmy Murphy, Mick Quinlan.

**Radio (Technical):-** Jack McGrath, Paddy Dowling, Bob Bolton, Bill McCarthy, Dan Looney; (AFTN):- Bill Roche, Kay O'Connell, Lena Howe, Jenny King, Eileen O'Sullivan, Johanna O'Connor.

**Meteorological Service:-** Michael Murtagh, Seán McAuliffe, Denis Cahill.

**Fire & Security Service:-** Gerry Tracey, Mick Doherty, Barry Roche, Garrett Aherne, Tom Russell, Willie O'Reilly, Mick McAuliffe, Christie Moriarty, Denis Maher, Donie Harris, Mick Healy, Jerry O'Brien, John Milner, Paddy Dempsey, Mick Staunton, Denis McSweeney, Pat Gallagher, Jerry Donovan.

**Customs (Preventive Officers):-** Seán O'Donnell, Tom Walsh; Joe McNally (Landing Side):-

**Immigration:-** Gerry Riordan.

**Post & Telegraphs:-** Dan Donovan.

**Agriculture:-** Sean McCarthy.

**Shell/BP:-** Joe Lynam, Jerry O'Donnell, Maurice Histon, Jim Condon.

**Taxis:-** Denis Desmond was the first taxi driver to serve Cork Airport and was there on opening day.

Tom Walsh
OIC Customs (Preventive

Bill Roche
Supervisor AFTN

Gerry Tracey
OIC Fire & Security Service

# 3

## CHAPTER THREE

After the airport opened, it was some time before the contractors finally left. For Resident Engineer, Brendan Clancy and Maintenance Foreman, Jack Walsh, there was much to be done to make the place presentable, including the laying of lawns and the landscaping of the approach from the main entrance. Later, many magnificent flower-beds were created. Credit for such displays was due to airport gardener, Mick O'Sullivan, and his able assistant Jim O'Sullivan. A viewing balcony was later built. It became a most important location for visitors and for those welcoming home or seeing off their loved ones.

It was expected that about 30,000 passengers would use the airport in its first full year of operation. It was a very conservative estimate. From opening day 16th October 1961 until 31st December, the figure was 10,246. The absence of catering facilities during the first few months posed problems, for both passengers and for staff. These facilities and a bar were ready in the spring of 1962. Great Southern Hotels, then the catering branch of CIE, got the franchise. The Catering Manager was Louis O'Hara.

In the early years, the airport had no public car park and motorists were allowed park on the south ramp free of charge. The main airlines serving Cork Airport in the early '60s were Aer Lingus and Cambrian Airways linking Cork

An Aer Lingus DC3 bound for Liverpool via Dublin being loaded with a cargo of shoes from the Cork Shoe Company towards the end of 1961.

L to R:- John Buckley, Jim Forde, Eddy Mullins, James Keane (all Aer Lingus); Maurice Histon and Jerry O'Donnell (Shell); Sean McCarthy (Dep. Of Agriculture).

*Photo – Courtesy John Buckley.*

## CORK AIRPORT WINTER SCHEDULE 1961
### Effective 1st November

| Airline | Type of Aircraft | Time Local Arr | Dept. | Route |
|---------|------------------|----------------|-------|-------|
| | | **MONDAY** | | |
| ALT. | F27 | 0945 | 1015 | Dublin/Cork/Paris |
| CAMBRIAN | DC3 | 1225 | 1540 | London/Cork/London |
| ALT. | F27 | 1255 | 1325 | Dublin/Cork/Cardiff/London |
| ALT. | F27 | 1645 | 1715 | Paris/Cork/Dublin |
| ALT. | F27 | 1910 | 1935 | London/Cardiff/Cork/Dublin |
| | | **TUESDAY** | | |
| ALT. | F27 | 0930 | 1000 | Dublin/Cork/Bristol/London |
| CAMBRIAN | DC3 | 1250 | 1540 | London/Cardiff/Cork/Cardiff/London. |
| ALT. | F27 | 1545 | 1610 | London/Bristol/Cork/Dublin. |
| | | **WEDNESDAY** | | |
| ALT. | F27 | 1255 | 1325 | Dublin/Cork/Cardiff/London. |
| CAMBRIAN | DC3 | 1250 | 1540 | London/Bristol/Cork/Bristol/London. |
| ALT. | F27 | 1910 | 1935 | London/Cardiff/Cork/Dublin. |
| | | **THURSDAY** | | |
| ALT. | F27 | 0930 | 1000 | Dublin/Cork/Bristol/London |
| CAMBRIAN | DC3 | 1225 | 1540 | London/Cork/London. |
| ALT | F27 | 1545 | 1610 | London/Bristol/Cork/Dublin. |
| | | **FRIDAY** | | |
| CAMBRIAN | DC3 | 1250 | 1540 | London/Cardiff/Cork/Cardiff/London |
| ALT | F27 | 1255 | 1325 | Dublin/Cork/London. |
| ALT | F27 | 1850 | 1935 | London/Cork/Dublin. |
| | | **SATURDAY** | | |
| CAMBRIAN | DC3 | 1250 | 1540 | London/Bristol/Cork/Bristol/London. |
| ALT | F27 | 1255 | 1325 | Dublin/Cork/London. |
| ALT | F27 | 1850 | 1935 | London/Cork/Dublin. |

### SUNDAY AIRPORT CLOSED

Cork Airport Police/Fire First Aid Certificate recipients 1962

Back Row L to R:- D. McSweeney, O. Kelly, D. Collins,T. Kerrigan, M. Staunton, P. Gallagher, J. O'Brien, M. Keohane. Middle Row L to R:- D Maher, W. O'Reilly, P. Dempsey, D. Harris, J. Millner, M. Healy, G. Ahern, M. McAuliffe. Seated L to R:- M.Doherty, Mrs. M. O'Sullivan (Red Cross), G. Tracey ,V. Fanning Airport Manager, G. Healy Lord Mayor of Cork, D. Minihan, S. Ryan.

*Photo – Aer Rianta Cork*

with Dublin, London, Paris, Bristol and Cardiff. Cambrian was a subsidiary of British European Airways (BEA) and operated to Cardiff, Bristol and London Heathrow all year round. The inaugural Cork-Paris scheduled service began on 20th October 1961 by an Aer Lingus Fokker F-27 (EI-AKC) and the first cargo flight to the airport was an Aer Lingus DC-3 from Dublin with 3.5 tons of freight on 22nd November 1961. Aer Lingus inaugurated the Cork-Birmingham route on 6th April 1962. Services to Lourdes and Barcelona were also opened that year, as well as a summer service to Exeter by Jersey Airlines using DC3s.

A number of smaller companies were granted licences to operate to Cork but only a few took up the option. Derby Airways had a service from Derby and Birmingham in 1962 while Starways of Liverpool, flew to Cork using DC-3 and DC-4 aircraft. Aer Lingus and Cambrian Airways covered the Liverpool route for some time towards the late 1960s and then discontinued. The Cork-Liverpool route, despite that city's great Irish connections, never proved a very successful venture.

To meet increasing demand, Aer Lingus used the bigger Viscount and Cambrian acquired them also. Cambrian operated them on the Cork-Heathrow route from April 1963 to April 1970; Cork-Liverpool April 1965 to September 1969; Cork-Manchester April 1967 to September 1968 and Cork–Cardiff/Bristol April 1966 to September 1968 and during the summer of 1969 and 1970. British United Airways (Channel Island) flew the Cork-Exeter route June to September 1965 to 1967 inclusive.

Some of the Airport Police/Fire Service in January 1962.
L to R:- Mick Doherty, Willy O'Reilly,Tom Russell, Donie Harris
Jerry O'Brien, Denis Maher.
*Photo – Courtesy Donie Harris*

Beside an FAA DC-3 flight check aircraft in June 1962.
L to R:- Donie Harris, Garret Ahern, Pat Gallagher.
*Photo – Courtesy Donie Harris*

# A Super Constellation Ditched in the Atlantic (1962).

Within a year of the opening, Cork Airport had its first involvement in a major air accident. On Sunday 23rd September 1962, an American Super Constellation of the Flying Tiger Airline was en route from McGuire Air Force Base, New Jersey to Frankfurt via Shannon Airport. On board were 59 U.S. army personnel, 7 adult dependants, 2 children aged 9 and 11 years and a crew of 8. About four hours out from Gander, Newfoundland, two of the plane's engines failed. As a precautionary measure, the stewardesses gave ditching instructions to the passengers. Matters became extremely serious when the third engine failed and plans were made to ditch the aircraft. The Captain's distress message was picked up at the RAF Air Traffic Control Centre at Prestwick.

By this time, the aircraft had been flying for about five hours and was a little more than half way to Frankfurt. Distress messages were sent out giving the plane's approximate position in the sea. One wing was broken on impact but the aircraft did not break up. However, the impact was enormous and many were seriously injured while others lost their lives. A Canadian Aircraft Carrier *Bonaventure* picked up the distress message at 9 pm when it was about 500 miles from the scene of the crash and had four destroyers dispatched to the area. Those who had survived the impact were on life rafts, many of them in a very serious condition. On receipt of the distress messages, rescue plans were immediately formatted and both RAF and USAF search aircraft took to the air.

Cars parked on the south ramp, March 1962. It was the era of the Ford Anglia
and Prefect cars . A Morris Mini Estate van is seen centre of picture.
*Photo – Gabriel Desmond*

An RAF Shackleton maritime patrol aircraft which was involved in the search
and rescue operations of the Flying Tiger Constellation, refuelling at Cork
Airport 26th Sept. 1962.
*Photo – Courtesy Bill Jestin*

The Swiss freighter *Celerina* arrived at the scene around 5am on Monday 24th September. Cork Airport rescue services were placed on full alert when it was learned that fourteen of the more seriously injured were being brought by the freighter close to the Cork coast for lift off by helicopter. The ship had picked up forty four survivors from a raft and was en route to Antwerp.

The airport opened at 0715 on Wednesday 26th September to facilitate rescue operations and was a scene of considerable activity. Two RAF Whirlwind rescue helicopters from RAF Chivenor in Devon landed for fuel at 0940 and took off again immediately. They were guided by an RAF Shackleton aircraft to rendezvous with the *Celerina* eight miles off Galley Head. Just before noon, the first of the survivors were landed by helicopter at Cork Airport and met by a team of doctors, nurses and ambulance men. They were rushed to the Mercy Hospital for treatment. All the injured had been taken to hospital by 1430. Later that day, nine of them were flown out to the US Army Hospital at Burderop Park near Swindon, Wiltshire. The remainder, including the navigator of the crashed plane, were suffering from second-degree burns and were kept in hospital overnight and flown the following day to the UK for further medical attention. When all the injured had been transferred, the *Celerina* continued on her way to Antwerp with the remainder of those it had rescued. The aircraft carrier *Bonaventure*, which had four survivors and three dead on board, proceeded to the Shannon Estuary where they were taken off.

It was Cork Airport's first grim reminder of the vital role it could be called on to play at any time and in this, its first such incident, its staff acquitted itself admirably. A poignant feature of the air crash was the death of the chief stewardess,

A Jersey Airline DC-3 which operated an Exeter-Cork service in Summer 1962.
*Photo –Gabriel Desmond*

Elizabeth Sims Cannin, who had only been married a month previously and was on her last flight with the airline.

- - -

The winter of 1962/63 was a very severe one with great snowfalls in January of 1963. The airport was badly affected and it was necessary to hire outside machinery to clear the runways of snow, which lay piled up for weeks.

During the early years, the airport was very quiet in the winter months and an enormous number of hares inhabited the airport lands. The Cork Coursing Club was granted permission to net them on Sunday mornings before the start of each season.

In 1962, 76,184 passengers used Cork Airport. Facilities, which were adequate when it opened, soon became overcrowded. It had cost £1.1 million, to build and the government were reluctant to spend more so soon after its construction.

In 1963, to prevent the possibility of aquaplaning by aircraft, it was found necessary to cut channels in the concrete at the intersection of the runways, so that rain-water, which lodged there could run off. The result was very satisfactory.

. The roll-on roll-off sea ferries hadn't yet come into operation and Aer Lingus began an air car-ferry business with the purchase of two ATL-98 Carvairs in 1963 and a further one in 1964. They were converted DC-4s. The conversion entailed lengthening the fuselage, fitting a taller tail and raising the flight deck to allow the loading of 5 cars through a nose door. . For loading, a scissors lift was used which was an awkward process. The Carvair had a compartment for 32 passengers at the rear. The aircraft, EI-AMP *St. Albert*, EI-AMR *St. Jarlath* and EI-ANJ *St. Senan* were used by Aer Lingus on the Dublin-Liverpool, Bristol-Cherbourg and Cork-Bristol routes. The latter route operated from June to October up to

Carvair car ferry plane during pilot training at Cork in April 1963
*Photo –Gabriel Desmond*

A BOAC Comet 4, G-APDI, was the first jet plane to land at Cork. It was operating an Aer Lingus flight from London on 31st July 1964.
*Photo – Gabriel Desmond*

1966. The British Civil Aviation Authority had granted a licence to Channel Airways to operate a car ferry service and Aer Lingus responded. The Carvairs were troublesome aircraft with poor reliability. Turnaround was slow and sometimes they were hours or even days late. Aer Lingus carried out pilot training at Cork airport in one of the Carvairs in April 1963 before they went into service.

President Kennedy's visit to Cork on Friday 28th June 1963 caused considerable airport activity. Although the President did not land at the airport, the visit brought an influx of U.S. military aircraft including two VH-34s before the visit. CH-34 and VH-3 USAF Sea King helicopters also arrived at the airport. As part of the very tight security involved, a specially checked tank of fuel had been provided, which was guarded on a 24-hour basis by American Military Police flown in from their base near Paris. The President travelled from Dublin by helicopter on the morning of 28th June and landed at Collins Barracks, Cork. His many aides, security men etc. travelled by other helicopters, all of which refuelled at the airport. Other aspects of security such as the risk of a terrorist attack were high on the list for the airport security staff. At the end of his visit, President Kennedy left for Dublin by helicopter from what is now Kennedy Park on Victoria Road.

The concessionaires at the airport in early 1964 were Aer Lingus, Irish Shell, Great Southern Hotels (Catering), Tom Moloney (Car Hire), International Contract Cleaners, Ulster Bank, T. Mullins (Souvenir Shop) and H. Walker (Fancy Goods and Newspapers).

The original Airport Bar in June 1964.
*Photo –Aer Rianta Cork*

The Airport Bar 2001.
*Photo – Aer Rianta Cork*

Starways, who operated the Cork-Liverpool route were taken over by British Eagle in 1964 and maintained the service until November 1968 when the airline went bankrupt.

In the early sixties, two Guinness Festival Clocks, which were a big attraction everywhere they went, toured Ireland and in June/July 1964 one was on display at the airport. It was located on the green across the road from the terminal. The Guinness Festival Clock was originally made for the Festival of Britain centenary celebrations in 1951 and made its first appearance in the Pleasure Gardens at Battersea that May. There it remained until 1953. The clock was 25 feet tall, weighed 1½ tons and was a marvel of engineering achievement. It was a huge attraction as every 15 minutes, weird creatures associated with the clock came to life. These creatures were widely featured in Guinness advertisements at that time. The clock was so successful that eight full size and one measuring 5 feet tall were made. They were withdrawn in October 1966 and sent for scrap.

The first jet to land at Cork Airport was a British Overseas Airways Corporation Comet 4, G-APDI, operating a London flight for Aer Lingus on 31st July 1964. Its arrival had been much publicised and large crowds flocked to the airport. The approach road was lined with cars and spectators crammed the upper balcony to get a good view.

Throughout its 40 years of operation, Cork Airport has maintained an excellent safety record. There has never been a fatal crash involving a commercial aircraft at the airport and only one fatal crash involving a private plane. There have been a number of incidents and tragedies, some of which engulfed the airport with anguish and sorrow but have also highlighted the important role the airport plays in such circumstances.

Guinness Festival Clock at the airport in July 1964
*Photo - Gabriel Desmond*

74

# Fatal Crash of Private Plane (1964).

The arrival from Southampton of a five-seater Piper Comanche aircraft on the evening of 7th August 1964 was just one more flight movement in the life of the airport. On board with the 33 years old English pilot James Coupe were Noel Looney of Sydney Park, Cork, Brian Gaule, a dentist from Youghal, based in London and his receptionist Miss Pilar Tuiz, a 24 years old Spaniard.

The following day, a pleasure flight was offered to the Gaule family. Patrick J. Gaule, who was then Manager of the Provincial Bank in Youghal, declined the offer but watched the take-off from the then balcony of the airport. His wife Maureen and sons Brian and John availed of the flight. Shortly after the plane was airborne and had reached a height of about one hundred feet, black smoke was seen to come from the engine. The pilot radioed the Control Tower for permission to return to the airfield, which was immediately granted. In carrying out this operation, the stricken plane went into a climbing turn and immediately lost power, after which it plunged to the ground killing all on board.

Mr. Patrick Gaule, who witnessed the tragedy from the airport balcony, was a native of Kilkenny and had served in the South Mall, Cork and in Schull as manager before coming to Youghal. His only daughter Phyllis was based in Dublin at the time of the tragedy and had she been home for the weekend, she too might have shared the same fate.

The Department of Transport and Power carried out an investigation into the crash. The Accident Report found that the probable cause was that the pilot had lost control of the aircraft in a turn following take-off. A contributory cause was partial or complete engine failure as a result of an over-rich mixture. It also noted that the pilot had a severe defi-

Piper PA-24 Comanche, seen at Cork Airport shortly before it
crashed on 8th August 1964. The four on board were killed.
*Photo – Gabriel Frost*

The Ilyushin 14M plane which brought the Bulgarian soccer team
to Cork in September 1964.
*Photo – Gabriel Desmond*

ciency in the movement of his right arm and there was evidence that he had difficulty in operating certain controls located to his right.

- - -

In September 1964 there was considerable excitement at the airport following the arrival of a Bulgarian Air Transport plane – a Russian built Ilyushin 14M. On board was a Bulgarian soccer team, which had come to play Cork Celtic. The visitors won by two goals to nil. Cork had drawn 0-0 with the Bulgarians in their away match. In later years, a number of Bulgarian flights in the larger Ilyushin 18 were made in connection with the Cork Choral Festival and with the rotation of ships' crews.

The only main change made to the terminal during the early years was the widening of the Arrivals Hall in 1965. In that year too, the Control Tower was double-glazed. This greatly improved the temperature problems experienced, especially in the winter and at the same time reduced the noise level for staff. In 1965 also, VASI (Visual Slope Indicator) lights were installed on Runway 25. These lights were an aid to aircraft making their approach to the runway touchdown point, especially in poor visibility. The pilot picked up a white light if the aircraft was at the correct angle of descent and a red light if the aircraft was at too low an angle.

The first jets ordered for Aer Lingus European routes were the BAC-1-11. On 30th May 1965, one of them made a promotional visit to Cork and took a group on a flight over Bantry Bay.

Because of the light air traffic schedule in the early years, Cork Airport was an ideal place for pilot training. One airline to avail of this was Caledonian Airways. In the spring of

Famous World War II RAF Fighter Pilot Douglas Bader at
Cork Airport September 1965
*Photo –Courtesy Irish Examiner*

1965 it had training sessions in Bristol Britannia aircraft, known as 'the whispering giant' because of its quiet engines. On 31st May 1965, Aer Lingus inaugurated a service between Cork and Manchester.

President De Valera landed at the airport on 24th July 1966 en route to Cape Clear where he opened an Irish College. He travelled to the island from the airport by an Air Corps Alouette helicopter and returned the following day.

- - -

In August 1966, sad scenes were witnessed at the airport following the arrival of the remains of Cork nun Sister Eamon O'Sullivan. She had been a missionary in Peking for 28 years and prior to being expelled by the Cultural Revolutionary Red Guards, had been brutally treated. She was then put on a baggage trolley and pushed across a railway bridge at Lo Wu on the border between China and Hong Kong. Within eighteen hours, she had died in a Hong Kong hospital. When the remains arrived at Cork airport, they were met by her relatives, who presented a crucifix to the Fire and Security personnel who assisted. A book on Sister Eamon (Molly O'Sullivan) called *The Bridge at Lo Wu* was written by Fr. Desmond Forrestal and was published in 1987.

- - -

There had been a continuous increase in passenger traffic since Cork airport opened in 1961 and by the end of 1966 the numbers had more than doubled to 160443. This posed problems, for the airlines who were under pressure to provide bigger aircraft on the routes serving Cork and also for airport management who saw that the terminal, airport ramp etc. had difficulty coping.

In the winter of 1966/67, over a three months period, channels were cut the full length of the main runway to carry

World War II aircraft at Cork Airport 6th June 1965 used in the making of the film The Blue Max.
*Photo –Courtesy Irish Examiner*

80

off rain-water. The channels covered the runway width to within 12.5 feet on either edge. It was a difficult and tedious job slicing through concrete and was carried out in extremely severe weather conditions. The work was made all the more difficult due to the fact that it had to be carried out at night when the airport was closed to traffic.

- - -

In February 1967, Vincent Fanning, who had been Cork Airport Manager since it opened in 1961 was transferred to Dublin Airport as Manager. Sadly, he died in November 1973 at the early age of 52. At that time, he was Director of Irish Airports. Paddy O'Grady replaced him in Cork. A flamboyant character, he was well known for walking to work in fine weather from his home in Bishopstown and back again in the evenings. He remained in Cork until his appointment as Chairman of International Services, Aer Rianta in September, 1973. On his retirement he went to live in Co. Galway.

- - -

The rapid increase in passenger traffic experienced at the airport from 1961 took a knock due to a serious outbreak of Foot and Mouth Disease in the UK in 1967. There were very rigid controls put into force for passengers travelling to and from Ireland. It was a familiar sight at the airport to see the footwear of all passengers from the UK being sprayed with disinfectant. The stringent restrictions led to a very considerable drop in passenger figures, especially in the first half of 1968. On 25th June, Britain was declared free from foot and mouth disease and traffic began to build up again. In 2001 events followed a similar pattern.

President deValera leaving the airport terminal 24th July 1966 en route to open an Irish College in Oileán Cléire. On his right is Seán Casey Lord Mayor of Cork and on his left is Vincent Fanning, Cork Airport Manager.

*Photo - Gabriel Desmond*

# Tuskar Rock Air Tragedy (1968).

On the morning of Sunday March 24th 1968 Aer Lingus Flight EI 712 from Cork to London was scheduled to depart at 1030. There was the usual bustle of activity as passengers with their luggage queued at the check-in counter while on the airport apron, ground engineers methodically carried out their routine inspection of the aircraft, registration EI-AOM and named *St. Phelim*.

The plane was a Viscount 803 built in 1957 by Vickers for KLM, the Dutch Airline. It had over 18,500 flying hours clocked up. Aer Lingus had bought it eighteen months previously. It had a seating capacity for 65 passengers and on that Sunday morning 57 had booked on the flight to London. There was a mixture of Irish, English and Continental travelling. Some were local such as Mrs. Burke, a member of the airport catering staff and the Catholic Chaplain to the airport, Rev. Fr. Hegarty C.C. Ballypehane, who was on his way to the Irish Centre in London to attend a social and dance being held there by former residents of Ballypehane.

Travelling on the flight to a conference in the UK were three staff members of the Agricultural Institute (now Teagasc), at Moorepark, Fermoy, Michael Cowhig, John Nyhan and Thomas Dwane. Among the passengers too were Rory Delaney, Barney O'Rourke and Kevin O'Callaghan of the Norwich Union Insurance Company Cork. On the previous night, when the curtain came down on the final performance of the show, *Oliver*, Mr. James N. Healy paid a glowing tribute to the musical conductor, William Cox-Ife. The Englishman, delighted with the show's success, said that he looked forward returning to the Cork Opera House at the first opportunity. He too was travelling on the flight.

Cars being unloaded on the south ramp from an Aer Lingus
Carvair Cork-Bristol-Cork in 1965.
*Photo – Courtesy John Buckley*

A Dan Air Airspeed Ambassador on a Ford's charter" to Cork' 8th August 1966.
The Ambassadors were also known as Elizabethens when they were in BEA
service.  One of them crashed taking off at Munich with the Man.United team
on board, 6th February 1958 killing twenty three.
*Photo – Gabriel Desmond*

Laden with fishing rods and tackle were nine Swiss anglers. They had been on a fishing holiday in Glenbeigh, Co. Kerry and were flying to London to connect with Swissair. Apart from the many Cork city people on the flight, there were those from neighbouring towns such as Cobh, Kinsale and Mallow. Also on board were two children-in-arms.

The Viscount's captain was Bernard O'Beirne who had celebrated his thirty fifth birthday two weeks previously. He was a native of Swinford, Co. Mayo and was a well-known amateur golfer. The first officer was twenty two years old Paul Heffernan of Ballintemple, Cork who was to receive his senior commercial pilot's licence the following week. The other two members of the crew were hostesses Ann Kelly from Wexford and Mary Coughlan of Ballykisteen, Co. Tipperary. The weather reports for the day showed fair weather and a surface visibility of 18 miles between Cork and the Tuskar Rock.

The Viscount Flight 712 took off from Cork Airport at 10.32 and began to climb as directed to 7000 feet, routing over Youghal. Within minutes the flight was handed over by Air Traffic Control at Cork to Shannon Control, who directed it to climb to flight level 170 (17,000 feet). By 10.38, Shannon had received clearance from London Airways for the Viscount to re-route direct to Strumble and they notified the Viscount accordingly. The aircraft acknowledged this. At 10.41 the aircraft notified Shannon that it was climbing through 9000 feet and at 10.51 the Viscount advised Shannon that it had levelled off at 17,000 and estimated to be over Strumble at 11.03. Shannon Control then instructed the Viscount at 10.56.30 to change to London Airways, Frequency 131.2 MHz. The aircraft replied "131.2".

An Taoiseach Jack Lynch, T.D. and Erskine Childers,T.D. Minister of Transport and Power, who arrived at Cork Airport to attend church ceremonies for the Tuskar Rock air crash victims of 28th March 1968, being escorted to the terminal by Cork Airport Manager Paddy O'Grady and Assistant Manager Gerry Holohan.

*Photo –Courtesy Irish Examiner*

At 10.58.02 London Radar received the following transmission from the aircraft – "Echo India Alpha Oscar Mike with you" followed in eight seconds by a further transmission – "Twelve thousand feet, descending, spinning rapidly". It was the last call from the stricken plane, which in a short space of time plunged into the sea off Tuskar Rack, killing all on board. A full scale alert was declared at 11.25 am.

Cork Airport was stunned when the news broke. By a twist of fate, Mrs. Burke of the airport catering staff was travelling with her elderly mother, Mrs. O'Callaghan. They were initially booked to fly out on Saturday morning but changed their flight to Sunday evening, later changing to the ill-fated morning flight. A Cork girl, who was with a touring party in Baltimore collapsed when she heard the news on radio of the tragedy. Her brother had booked on the morning flight to London or so she thought. In fact, he had changed his mind at the last minute and booked an evening flight instead. Three Germans, Klaus Haas, Gerd Hoffmeyer and Helmut Voso, who had been making a travel film on County Cork, missed death when their hired car broke down on their way to the airport. Others were not so lucky. Air hostess, Mary Coughlan, had changed flights with another hostess and Michael Cowhig and a colleague had changed places on the London trip.

The airport switchboard was soon jammed with callers. Anxious relatives flocked to the airport, many in a very distressed state. A stream of public representatives, clergy etc. including the Lord Mayor, Mr. Pierce Wyse came and paid their respects as by mid-afternoon wreckage was sighted. By then, local, UK and European press was at the airport. The gravity of the disaster as it unfolded had a numbing affect on everyone.

An investigation by the Irish Air Accident Investigation Unit was carried out and was published in 1970. The exact cause of the accident was never established. Of the 12 conclusions reached in the Report, one was the subject of much discussion and public controversy.

*There is evidence which could be construed as indicative of the possible presence of another aircraft or airborne object in the vicinity which, by reason of collision, or by its proximity causing an evasive manoeuvre to be made, or by its wake turbulence, might have been the initiating cause of an upsetting manoeuvre resulting in the Viscount entering a spin or spiral dive.*

*There is no substantiating evidence of such a possibility, but it cannot be excluded for it is compatible with all of the presently available evidence.*

*Under the heading 'Probable Cause' the Report found:*

*There is not enough available evidence on which to reach a conclusion of reasonable probability as to the initial cause of this accident.*

*The probable cause of the final impact with the sea was impairment of the controllability of the aircraft in the fore and aft (pitching) plane.*

Speculation that the Viscount may have been hit by a missile or by an unmanned craft grew as time went by.

In his book *Tragedy at Tuskar Rock* published in 1983, the author Dermot Walsh wrote as follows:

The long list of unanswered questions about the crash of EI-AOM demand further investigation. The accident inspector's enduring but unsupported by evidence conviction that the plane was struck; the co-incidental proximity to the scene of the crash of British naval vessels, their rush to the scene and the

Famous film star Charlie Chaplin with his wife Oonagh pictured
outside Harry Walker's Shop at Cork Airport 8th April 1968.
*Photo – Courtesy Irish Examiner*

subsequent strong involvement of the British naval authorities in the search and salvage operation allied to the evidence of 'remarkable' witnesses of another aircraft in the sky over Wexford at the time of the crash, plus the other puzzling elements of the mystery crash require in-depth and adequately funded probing.

That a component of the tail assembly was found many miles from the area of the crash enhanced the missile or another aircraft theory. However, there were others not so convinced and perhaps there was another reason. In his book *The Flight of the Iolar*, the author Bernard Share wrote in reference to the Tuskar Rock air tragedy:

"In the absence of any countervailing evidence, the missile theory remained a possible hypothesis, though there were many, Arthur Walls and Dick White amongst them, who inclined to the view that the accident had been caused by structural failure."

Arthur Walls, who was Assistant General Manager of Aer Lingus, lost his brother Desmond Peter Walls in the incident. Dick White was a former Aer Lingus pilot, later becoming Chief Operations Officer.

Calls for a re-opening of the investigation intensified over the years. They were backed up by newspaper articles, television and radio programmes etc, which focused on the possible involvement of UK ships and missile ranges on the Welsh Coast in the downing of the *St. Phelim*. As a result, on the thirtieth anniversary of the accident, the U.K. Ambassador to Ireland met with relatives of the victims of the *St. Phelim* and offered to assist them in establishing the exact nature of the role of the UK Ministry of Defence in the accident.

Three members of the Cork Airport Annual Dinner Dance Committee 1968.
L to R:- Mick O'Sullivan, Joe O'Connor, Dermot Collins.
*Photo – Courtesy Dermot Collins*

The Minister for Public Enterprise, Mrs. Mary O'Rourke, T.D. also met with the UK Ambassador and it was jointly agreed that Irish and UK officials would review all files held relating to the accident to see if the cause could be established. This Review was published in mid 2000. Many of the issues raised over the years were clarified but also the maintenance history and Maintenance Operating Errors of EI-AOM were found by the Minister for Enterprise to be "disturbing".

The Review report stated that the involvement of the UK authorities assuming initial responsibility for the search of the crashed Viscount *St. Phelim* was because the initial indications were that the aircraft had come down in the UK flight zone. It was pointed out that the State did not have a Naval Service sufficiently equipped to adequately resource a Search and Rescue effort of the level of Operation Tuskar nor did the State have the material resources to recover the wreckage of the *St. Phelim* from the sea-bed.

The UK Ships that first arrived in the Search area, *HMS Penelope* and *HMS Hardy* were not missile equipped and provided humanitarian assistance under International Search and Rescue Procedures. The Review also concluded that the use of Royal Navy Ships to recover the *St. Phelim* from the sea bed presented the best and possibly the only solution to the requirement. It was also felt that the lack of financial commitment on the part of the State to indefinitely fund the Search and Salvage operation may have contributed to its limited success.

The Review concluded that the UK position had not changed since the time of the accident with regard to missile ranges being closed on the day of the crash and that there were no naval or other military exercises on that day.

Fred Astaire at Cork Airport 14th July 1969 being escorted by Aer Lingus
Ground Hostess Margaret Kelly. At rear is Tess Ronan, also of Aer Lingus.
*Photo – Courtesy Irish Examiner*

Referring to the 1970 Report , the Review stated:

*The report should have included or referred to the fault rectification and maintenance problems identified in the post crash inspection as contained in the Departmental File submitted to this review.*

*There were serious errors in the Maintenance Plan of EI-AOM at the time of the accident.  These errors originated within Aer Lingus.*

*The omission from the Final Report of details of the aircraft's maintenance history, except in the briefest of terms, is difficult to comprehend.*

*The total omission, from the Final Report, of details of the errors in EI-AOM's Maintenance Operating Plan is difficult to comprehend.*

*While the maintenance history and Maintenance Operating Plan errors of EI-AOM  contain many matters for concern, there is no evidence that any of these items had a bearing on the cause of the accident.*

However, the Minister for Public Enterprise found the findings with regard to maintenance records of EI-AOM "deeply disturbing" and decided to appoint two international air crash investigators to reopen the files in connection with that part of the findings.  There the matter rests for the present.

- - -

It has already been stated that the airport opened under the control of and management by the State, the relevant department being Transport and Power.   That situation remained until 1st April 1968 when management functions were vested in Aer Rianta.   However, a transfer of Department personnel to Aer Rianta didn't begin until 1970. The staff who transferred from State services (Civil Service)

An aerial view of Cork Airport, September 1969. In later years, the terminal
was extended left of picture i.e. northwards.
*Photo - Gabriel Desmond*

A de Havilland Trident of Channel Airways seen at Cork on 1st July 1969 in connection with the opening of the Gulf Oil Terminal at Whiddy Island, Bantry Bay.
*Photo – Gabriel Desmond*

to Aer Rianta were from Airport Management, Engineering/Maintenance and Fire/Security. This situation will be dealt with in greater detail later.

On 1st June 1968, the first scheduled all night opening began. President Heinrich Lübke of West Germany and his wife arrived at Cork Airport on 5th September 1968. They were on their way to spend a holiday at the Hotel Europe in Killarney. The party came in a German Air Force Convair 340 and were met by the Taoiseach, Jack Lynch, the Airport Manager, Paddy O'Grady, the Federal German Ambassador to Ireland and Dan Cullinane, Honorary German Consul in Cork.

It was in 1968 also that British Eagle, who had taken over the Cork – Liverpool route from Starways in 1964, ceased operations and went into Liquidation. The airline had been one of the first to change from Viscounts to BAC 1-11s.

A very well kept secret was the arrival at the airport of General Charles de Gaulle on 10th April 1969 and took many people by surprise. There were strict security arrangements as the party left quietly for Heron Cove Hotel near Parknasilla. The airport had greatly recovered from the UK outbreak of Foot and Mouth disease in 1967/68 and by the end of 1969 passenger figures had reached 173,333.

The transfer of State staff to Aer Rianta began in 1970. There was much to be done. The airport had been opened in October 1961 and little development or expansion had taken place since then although the passenger figures had doubled. There never have been scheduled air services from the USA to Cork but on the morning of 27th August 1970, three Aer Lingus Boeing 707s were diverted to the airport due adverse weather at Shannon and Dublin. The aircraft were from Boston, New York and Chicago. On 1st April 1971 the Bank

To relieve congestion on the original airport stairs, which was on the left as one entered the terminal, a 'temporary' stairs, shown here, was provided at the end of the 1960s. This remained until 1993 when it was replaced under Phase 4 of the Passenger Terminal Development by an escalator, two panoramic lifts and a new stairs.

*Photo – Aer Rianta Cork*

of Ireland replaced the Ulster Bank, which had operated at the airport since it opened.

Cork airport, which relies very much on UK passenger traffic, suffered rather badly in the early 1970s due to the Northern troubles. The violence, following the reintroduction of internment in Northern Ireland in early August 1971, and the events of Bloody Sunday on 30th January 1972, when 13 civilians were killed by British Paratroops followed by the burning of the British Embassy in Dublin, dealt a shattering blow to the UK traffic at Irish airports. It took a considerable time for that traffic to build up again.

The first major development at Cork Airport under the new Aer Rianta management was in 1972 when an extension to the Fire Station was carried out. This included the construction of a new watch room, office and staff accommodation. Space was also made available for larger fire tenders coming on stream. It was also found necessary to extend the airport water supply, build a new reservoir and install new piping etc. Due to international security reasons, the balcony was closed to the general public in that year too and the pool beneath was filled in.

A series of charter flights from Amsterdam during the summer months by KLM Royal Dutch Airlines began in 1972 and were to last until 1982. A Duty Free shop was opened at Cork on 8th September 1972 and first to avail of the facility was an Aer Lingus flight from Cork to Amsterdam. As an extra landing aid, VASI Lights were installed on the main runway 17/35 in 1973. They had already been installed on the short runway 07/25 in 1965.

The first of the Boeing 737 jet aircraft which Aer Lingus took delivery of for its UK and European routes. The plane EI-ASA spent many days pilot training at Cork Airport in May 1969.

*Photo – Gabriel Desmond*

# Rescue of Pisces III Mini-Submarine (1973)

Rescue operations off our shores are a regular occurrence. One of the most dramatic and which involved major aviation activity at Cork Airport for several days was that of a miniature submarine, *Pisces III*, at the end of August 1973.

The 19 feet long midget submarine, which weighed 11 tons, had been laying a 30 miles length of submarine cable in a trench, about 94 miles southwest of Mizen Head. A fault developed and trapped the submarine on the seabed at a depth of 1400 feet. The crew of two were Englishmen Roger Chapman and Roger Mallison. The mother ship *Vickers Voyager IV* was near at hand on the surface when the distress call was picked up and immediately initiated a massive rescue operation. It was extremely serious as the men had only a limited supply of oxygen.

Cork Airport became the rescue base to which large amounts of equipment and personnel would be flown and it operated on a 24 hour basis throughout the rescue. On the morning of 30th August, two mini-submarines *Pisces II* and *Pisces V* were flown in. The latter was a three-man craft brought from Halifax, Nova Scotia in a Royal Canadian Air Force C-130 Hercules. *Pisces II* was on board another Hercules. A team of diving experts, led by the General Manager of Vickers Oceanic also arrived in the Company's jet.

Meanwhile the mother ship *Vickers Voyager IV* had berthed at Cork to pick up the mini-submarines, brought by road from the airport. Irish Helicopters, then engaged with Esso oil-drilling operations, received an urgent call from Vickers Oceanic Ltd. seeking assistance with the transfer of an expert who had arrived from Hydrodynamics Ltd. Vancouver, to the mother ship which was then on her way with the two

The Viewing Balcony at Cork Airport, which was a popular facility in the first decade of the airport's operations, was closed in the early '70s for security reasons and the pool beneath it was filled in.

*Photo – Aer Rianta Cork.*

Three Aer Lingus Boeing 707s from the US which were diverted to Cork 27th August 1970 due fog at Dublin and Shannon.

*Photo - Geoffrey Farrar*

mini-submarines to the rescue area. Irish Helicopters picked up the expert from the airport and in a very delicate operation put him on board the *Vickers Voyager IV* , which was proceeding at full speed 4 miles south-west of Daunt's Rock so that no time would be lost. The weather was then deteriorating and gale force winds were forecast.

When the rescue area had been reached, *Pisces II* was lowered and began its dive. Within a few hours it had located the stricken vessel on the seabed but failed to attach a cable. By now, the weather had deteriorated further. *Pisces V* with its three-man crew was then launched. Having found the stricken craft they succeeded in connecting a light line to it so that *Pisces II* could find its way down with a ten inch lifting cable.

In the meantime, a robot *Curv III*, capable of accurately pinpointing the location of an object at the bottom of the sea, was flown with other equipment to Cork Airport in two United States Air Force C-141A Starlifter planes. Accompanying the robot was a crew of eight under the command of project manager, Capt. Huntley Boyd, U.S. Navy Supervisor of Salvage. The arrival of *Curv III* gave new hope as an earlier model was used in the recovery of a hydrogen bomb lost off Palmores, Spain in 1966. It was rushed by road to Cork docks where a barge was waiting to take it to a back-up rescue ship *John Cabot*. When *Curv III* arrived at the quay side, the awaiting barge was found to be too small to carry the robot and a larger one was then supplied by the Cork Harbour Commissioners. Despite the delay, the robot found the midget submarine on Saturday 1st September and succeeded in attaching a cable to it. Then, the *John Cabot* slowly winched it from the sea bed. All was well with the crew of two. It was later discovered that the accident to the midget

Lord Mayor Alderman Peter Barry, T.D. pictured with Apollo 13 Astronauts James A.Lovell, John L. Swiglot and Fred. W. Haise before boarding a U.S. Air Force plane from Cork Airport to Shannon on 14th Oct. 1970.

*Photo - Courtesy Donal Harris*

In 1970, the late Pat Walsh (RIP), Airport Police/Fire Service and
Yvonne Roche, Information Assistant.
*Courtesy – Yvonne Whitley*

Brendan Clancy B.E. pictured at his departure presentation at Cork Airport December 1970. Back Row L to R:-Gerry Holohan, Asst. Apt. Manager Cork, Jim O'Sullivan, Exec. Asst. to GM Aer Rianta, J. Vincent Feehan, Chief Airports Engineer, Vincent Fanning , Manager Dublin Apt. Mick O'Sullivan, Gardener Cork Apt., Derek Keogh, Exec. Asst. to Aer Rianta GM, Joe O'Connor Duty Manager. Front Row L to R:- R. C. O'Connor, General Manager Aer Rianta, Brendan Clancy, Mrs. Deirdre Clancy, Paddy O'Grady, Manager Cork Apt.

*Photo – Courtesy Brendan Clancy*

submarine was caused by a rope, which had fouled the hatch-opening lever. This caused flooding of the craft's rear compartment, causing it to lie on the sea- bed. It was a very successful rescue and one in which Cork Airport staff played an important role.

- - -

In September 1973, Gerry Holohan, who had been assistant to the airport manager since Cork airport was opened, replaced Paddy O'Grady as airport manager. The latter had taken command in 1967 and served through the formative years of Aer Rianta's management. He left Cork on promotion to Manager International Services, Aer Rianta Dublin.

In 1975, Aer Rianta Technical Services undertook a passenger terminal development study for Cork Airport, which was aimed at improving the terminal facilities. In the course of the study and following discussions with local management, it was seen that the demand for office accommodation had far outstripped what was then available. Representations had already been made by business interests in Cork City and by airline operators with a view to having the facilities improved.

The study group, in their investigations, chose the period 1966 to 1974 at the airport as representative. During that time there was an average increase of 10,000 passengers per year, and if such trends were to continue, then the facilities available could be totally outstripped by the demand. Jet aircraft such as the B.737 and the BAC 1-11 were by then in use at the airport. Aer Rianta, therefore, embarked on a development and expansion programme. The Technical Services study showed that the current requirements could be met without embarking on a new major building programme by rationalising the traffic flow, modernising the baggage handling

Group taken at the presentation by Gerry Holohan, newly appointed Airport Manager, to former Manager Paddy O'Grady on his transfer to Dublin, September 1973.

*Photo – Aer Rianta Cork*

Two Lockheed C-141A Starlifters of the United States Air Force flew directly from the States to Cork Airport with rescue equipment for the recovery of the Pisces III mini-submarine and its crew of two from the sea south west of the Mizen Head in August 1973.

*Photo – Gabriel Desmond*

arrangements and utilising space to a maximum. The main problems found in the ground floor area were:

(a) The check-in counters were located too close to the arrivals area.

(b) The absence of carousel type baggage handling equipment was slowing up the processing of passengers through the baggage hall.

(c) The absence of a red and green channel system of customs examination extended the time arriving passengers were in the terminal building.

(d) The lack of an adequately sized Departure Hall.

The first floor layout didn't affect the passenger flow to the same extent as the ground floor so major alterations were not necessary there. To accommodate the renovations and alterations on the ground floor, the old departure, check-in and arrival areas disappeared. The bank and shopping areas were relocated. New departure and arrival halls, check-in area and office complex, information desk and duty office and a VIP Room were provided. These extensions and changes were substantial and proved to be of enormous benefit to an expanding airport.

Arising from all this, a new Duty Free Shop with more space and greater choice of goods was opened on 18th December 1977.

At the official opening of the completed extensions etc. on 29th June 1978, the Taoiseach, Mr. Jack Lynch said:

"The airport is an important asset both for tourism and commerce. It provides a natural gateway for tourists to Ireland's southwest, a region of outstanding natural beauty and of great attraction to travellers from abroad. An airport convenient to the major tourist destinations has obvious advantages,

Sean Ryan, C.A.S.O. making a presentation on behalf of the AP/FS to Paddy O'Grady former Airport Manager on the occasion of his transfer to Dublin in September 1973. Also in picture are L to R:- Ger Leonard, Sean McSweeney, Dermot Collins, John Lyons, Tom Kerrigan,Tom Breathnac, Mick McAuliffe, John O' Mahony, Pat Walsh, John Sexton. At Back Centre – Miah Keohane.

*Photo – Aer Rianta Cork*

Guarding the Bank in 1975!
L to R:- Miah Keohane, John O'Mahony, Pat Walsh (RIP).
*Photo- Aer Rianta Cork.*

Photo of Aviation Engineering Services team, winners of Cork Airport
Inter-Departmental Quiz Jan. 1975. Standing at rear L to R:- Caoimhin O
Donnchadha, Alan Roche. Seated L to R:-Terry Donovan, Sheila Barry, Tom
Clancy.
*Photo – Courtesy Tom Clancy*

both for the tourist himself and for the tourist developer, whether that developer be a national or local body."

Gerry Holohan, Airport Manager, said that he was grateful to the contractors and workers in this project, for completing the work without any disruptions of airport operations.

"Our airport is now capable of giving efficient and comfortable service to our air travellers and we hope that by 1985, we will be seeking further additions to our terminal."

- - -

In the airport's early years, there were petrol pumps close to the exit from the main car park. They went into disuse during the first oil crisis and were removed in 1977 together with the toll booth, which was operated by car park attendants until an automatic system was installed. The staff car park was also enlarged in 1978. However, that car park is now part of the short-term passenger car park and a new staff car park was opened above it.

On Saturday 1st July 1978, members of the Dutch Royal family arrived at Cork Airport. Among the group were Crown Prince Claus, Crown Princess Beatrix and their children. They were en route to Sneem, Co. Kerry to spend a holiday in the home of Mr. and Mrs. Raymond Roche. They were joined on the 21st July by Queen Juliana, who also flew into the airport.

Group on Dan Air inaugural flight Cardiff/Bristol/Cork seen here at
Cork Airport 6th April 1977.
*Photo –Courtesy Irish Examiner*

114

Jack Charlton, former Republic of Ireland Soccer Manager, pictured
In jovial mood by his sculpture at the indoor fish pond in the
terminal building at Cork Airport
*Photo – Michael McSweeney Pro Vision Photography*

# The Whiddy Island Disaster (1979)

The inferno at Whiddy Island on the night of 7th January 1979 created intense light aircraft activity at Cork Airport. A fire had developed on board the shuttle tanker Betelguese, which then exploded in a blast that was felt 12 miles away. Forty three French crew members and eight others died in the disaster. Cork Airport became the focal point, as Royal Navy, Irish Helicopters and Irish Air Corps involved in the search and rescue refuelled there. The accident, which was tragic and devastating in its intensity, showed how important it was to have the southern capital served by its own airport.

- - -

President Julius Nyerere of Tanzania, while on a state visit to Ireland, came to Cork airport on 19th September 1979.

- - -

From 1969 to 1979 passenger numbers doubled to 348,538.

Well known film actress Charlotte Rampling was at Cork Airport in 1977 for the shooting of a scene at the airport for the film The Purple Taxi. She is seen here with Irene Falvey, Aer Lingus Ground Hostess.

*Photo – Courtesy Irene Falvey*

# 4

## CHAPTER FOUR

As well as the changes in the terminal, it was necessary to extend the main apron in 1980 and the erection of the first phase of a new security fence began. The final phase was completed in 1987. Renovations were carried out to the Cargo Terminal and a new In-flight Catering Kitchen was also built in 1980.

The President of the German Federal Republic, Karl Karstens and his wife were at the airport on 1st May 1980. He had been on a three-day official visit to Ireland and on the day of his departure, he paid a visit to Glengariff. From there he was flown by helicopter to Cork Airport and brought by road to Cork City Hall for an official reception. On his return to the airport, from where he left for Germany in a Luftwaffe Boeing 707, President and Mrs. Hillery met him. On the tarmac was a military guard of honour from Ballincollig Barracks and the First Field Artillery Regiment fired a 21-gun salute. The Band of the Southern Command played and Irish Air Corps jets provided a fly over. Three large Sikorsky CH-53G helicopters of the German Army supported the presidential visit and made many flights between Cork, Baldonnel, West Cork and Killarney.

A national strike of Aer Lingus mechanics and maintenance personnel took place on 30th May '80. It was due to a

A snowy January morning at the airport in 1977. The terminal is
being extended on the right. The small staff car park is in front.
*Photo – Gabriel Desmond*

A DC-6 of the French cargo airline SFAIR, flying out
with calves, 1st July 1978.
*Photo – Gabriel Desmond*

pay relativity problem, which had arisen, following the settlement of grading and pay progression of operatives and clerks in the company. The strike ended on 4th July.

Dan Air inaugurated a Cork-Gatwick service on 13th April 1981. Among the eminent people to arrive at the airport that year was the former West German Chancellor, Willi Brandt on 2nd June.

On 13th January 1982, a private airline, Avair, commenced a commuter service between Cork and Dublin using 33 seat Shorts 330s aircraft. The company also operated a 19-seater Beechcraft, which was pressurised. Avair later ceased operations. Aer Lingus pilots, fearing job losses at this time, encouraged the company to form a commuter division by reverting to the use of smaller propeller planes suited to the short and less busy routes. Accordingly, two Shorts 330 planes were leased by Aer Lingus and took over the Cork Dublin service in 1984. They later used Shorts 360s.

In 1982, Cork Airport tackled the lack of facilities for the disabled, which had created problems for many pilgrims to Lourdes and other places. A new lift for invalids, together with toilets and first aid room were installed. High mast flood lighting of the apron areas was also completed in 1982. There had been a steady increase in passenger traffic in the '70s, especially in the latter half of the decade but the early '80s were years of recession and passenger traffic decreased. There was a drop of 35,000 between the end of 1979 and that of 1982. However, it gradually increased and in 1985 the figures equalled those of 1978 and from then on, as we shall see later, the passenger figures escalated.

Increased airport business brought its car parking difficulties, making it necessary to enlarge the main car park in 1983 and again in 1986. The latter extension took in an area of

Donal Cashman, President I.F.A. about to board an Aer Lingus Boeing 737 at Cork Airport for Brussels on 5th May 1980. Seeing him off are from left –Brendan Cronin, newly appointed Aer Lingus District Manager, Irene Falvey, Ground Hostess and Kevin Murphy, Senior Sales representative, Aer Lingus Cork.

*Photo - Courtesy Irene Falvey*

The Minister for Transport, Albert Reynolds T.D. with Aer Rianta staff members at Cork Airport in June 1980 - L to R Tom Russell, Billy Barry, Ann Mackesy, Stephanie Kenneally, Padraig Flynn T.D., Minister of State, Dept.of Transport, Teresa Ward, Paddy Dempsey.

*Photo –Aer Rianta Cork*

land, which had been known as "The Devil's Field".  The airport also needed a mortuary to cater for remains flown in for burial in Ireland.  To alleviate the stress on those sad occasions, one was built in 1983.

## Secret Rescue Mission (1983).

On the evening of 6th July, Cork Airport was the base for a very secret rescue mission being undertaken about 250 miles south west of Ireland, following a request from the Marine Rescue Co-ordination Centre at Shannon to have its rescue services mobilised.  The incident involved a U.S. nuclear submarine whose identity the Americans were anxious to hide. Accordingly, information was scant but it was made known that a crew member was suspected of having suffered a heart attack.

The U.S. Air Force took complete charge of the planned lift off of the man in question from the submarine. Cork Airport was placed on alert for the arrival of two HH-53 Helicopters together with two HC-130 Hercules long-range cargo planes on the following morning.  A total of 34 crew was involved in the air-side of the operation.  Eventually the sick man, Chief Petty Officer George Williamson was taken off the submarine and brought to the airport by helicopter. There, he was met by an ambulance and taken to the Cork University Hospital, where he was detained for some time. The HH-53 helicopters involved in the mission had a very long range and were capable of being refuelled in flight. This operation in fact took place at 6000 feet over Cork during the course of the rescue mission.

- - -

When the airport was built, a section of the terminal building carried a second floor, known as the Penthouse.

Avair,a private airline, began commuter services between Cork and Dublin in 1982 using 33 seat Shorts 330s, one of which is seen at Cork, 1st April '82.

*Photo – Gabriel Desmond*

Aer Rianta staff party at Metropole Hotel for the airport's 21st anniversary 16th October 1982. L to R:- Marie and Michael McAuliffe, Betty and Miah Keohane, Veronica O'Callaghan, Tim Murphy.

*Photo – Courtesy Tim Murphy*

Originally, it had been considered as an area suitable for a restaurant but the idea was quashed due lack of toilets on that floor. In 1984, the Penthouse was upgraded and its accommodation converted into offices, staff areas etc.

- - -

Gerry Holohan retired as Airport Manager in March 1984 and Barry Roche took over. Barry Roche had been on the airport staff since it opened, joining as a member of the Airport Police/Fire Service. He became Section Leader the following year. During his time in that Service, he took a B.A. degree at UCC. Following the changeover from State management to Aer Rianta, he transferred to Airports Administration and became a Duty Manager. He served as Commercial Manager for some time before his appointment as Airport Manager.

- - -

As part of the stringent security, so necessary at airports, the installation of closed circuit television cameras on top of the control tower at Cork was carried out in 1985. The cameras survey the entire airport area and relay their pictures to the airport security service.

Following the first major extension and development of the terminal in 1976, the next decade saw a phenomenal increase in passenger traffic. The terminal was gradually becoming congested again and not capable of providing a quality facility for passengers. Aer Rianta carried out a study of the situation in 1985. As a result, it was decided to embark on a major expansion and development programme, to be carried out in phases. The team behind the new Terminal design was Aer Rianta Technical Consultants (ARTC). From the project's inception, the man responsible was Project Manager-Architecture, Tony Kelly, who worked under Manager-Architecture, Barry Drinan. Also involved was the

A United States Air Force HH-53 Helicopter about to engage its refuelling probe in the hose and drogue trailing from the wing pod of a HC-130 Hercules, at 6000 feet over Cork on 1st August 1983
*Photo - Gabriel Desmond*

Retiring Airport Manager Gerry Holohan handing over the keys of power to incoming Manager Barry Roche in March 1984
*Photo – Courtesy Ray Shanahan.*

design team of Vincent Convery and Eamon O'Sullivan, while Paul O'Connor came on board during Phase III. Tom Fitzgerald was Clerk of Works for three of the four phases.

## Air India Disaster (1985)

Cork Airport became the focus of world media attention on Sunday 23rd June 1985 and for some time afterwards when it became the operational centre for a search and rescue operation in connection with a missing Air India aircraft.

The Boeing 747-237B Flight 182 was flying from Toronto, Canada to London on Sunday 23rd June. At 08.13 hours London time while flying at 31,000 feet it was about to enter Shannon Control airspace and call the Air Traffic Control Centre. Moments later, the aircraft disappeared from the radar screen without any warning or Mayday call. Unknown to the Control staff, Flight 182 had disintegrated in mid air and crashed into the sea off the south coast of Ireland. All 329 people on board perished. Following its disappearance, Shannon Marine Rescue Service immediately raised the alarm and a full-scale search and rescue operation was initiated. Within a few hours Cork Airport had become the scene of unprecedented activity.

Following the alert of RAF rescue centres, four Sea Kings and three Chinooks from the UK were dispatched to the scene. A large American helicopter from one of its bases there also came to assist. Very soon, news came through that many bodies were seen in the water in the vicinity of the crash area. Preparations had already been made by the airport's Police/Fire Service to receive the bodies lifted from the sea and rows of stretchers were laid out on the south ramp. The first of the Sea King Helicopters with several bodies on board touched down at 3 p.m. The remains were collected by

128

Horses being exercised on the ramp at Cork prior to boarding a Hercules C-130 of the Algerian Air Force, 17th May 1985.
*Photo – Gabriel Desmond*

Airport Security Officers Jim Hyland and Kevin Farrell keep the world press at bay in the aftermath of the Air India disaster over the Atlantic in June 1985.
*Photo – Courtesy Ray Shanahan*

the army's 1st Field Medics in Cork and later removed to the University Hospital.

All through Sunday the helicopters flew in and out, stopping only to unload recovered bodies and refuel. In the early afternoon, a large consignment of body bags was flown in. Of the first 70 victims recovered and brought to the airport, 54 were women and children. By late evening, large sections of the world press had arrived at the airport, which put enormous pressure on the phone lines. To alleviate this, telephone engineering staff provided 30 extra exchange lines and 5 telex lines. Through the assistance of an Bórd Telecom, RTE Cork Engineering staff, the Department of Communications and the Government Information Service under Mr. Joe Jennings, first class television, radio and telephone communications were made possible to many parts of the world as events unfolded.

The search for bodies went on until dark and resumed at first light on the following day. The Irish Air Corps and Irish Helicopters provided operational support for the very exhausted rescue crews. As the search resumed, the airport staff experienced great pressures as press and camera men jostled for vantage points from which to get their stories. The increased demands on the airport catering services were very efficiently handled by Harringtons. Airport staff had to cope with normal flight operations as well as those generated by the rescue services.

Shortly after 8 a.m. on Monday, the Taoiseach, Garrett Fitzgerald arrived to be briefed on the situation. He later gave a press conference. Overnight, the airport restaurant had been transformed into a press- room. Irish aviation experts, led by Vincent Feehan, Chief Executive Air Navigation Services and Gerry McCabe, Chief Aeronautical

A Canadair Challenger of the Canadian Armed Forces arrived at Cork with VIPs two weeks following the Air India disaster. Here the visitors are being greeted by Barry Roche, Airport General Manager.

*Photo – Gabriel Desmond*

Officer (Air Worthiness) also arrived to begin preliminary investigations. Cork Airport had been chosen as the base for them and in the days that followed, plane wreckage, which had been recovered, was delivered in army trucks under Garda supervision. Air India Engineers and maintenance experts as well as the Irish officials were all based at the airport.

The *Cork Evening Echo* described events at the airport on the morning following the disaster as follows:

This morning, the scenes at Cork Airport were reminiscent of war zone pictures from Vietnam. One international news correspondent compared it to Dan Nang airport at the height of the Vietnamese battles. A stream of helicopters ferrying corpses from the crash site flew to and from the airport, which has been turned into the operations centre for the search off the coast. Armed guards patrolled the runways and teams of news and camera-men from the world media took over the passenger restaurant which has become the nerve centre of press communications.

Further poignant scenes were witnessed at the airport on Tuesday 25th June when the first of the relatives of those killed in the crash arrived. They had come in defiance of an Air India appeal not to travel because of the condition of many of the bodies. Over 50 Cork families offered accommodation to the grieving relatives.

Cork Airport staff acquitted themselves magnificently in handling the enormous operational involvement of all the services concerned. When the initial activity had ceased, much work went on behind the scenes by the various national and international officials concerned who were based at

The memorial in the West Cork village of Ahakista commemorating the
325 people who perished in the Air India air disaster 23rd June 1985.
*Photo – Aer Rianta Cork*

In 1983 at Cork Airport:- L to R:- Edmond Forrest (Duty Free Store Manager), Gerry Holohan (Airport Manager), Barra O'Tuama (Aer Rianta Director), Jack Riordan (Airport Engineer), Jim Mitchell T.D. (Minister for Transport), Peter Hanley (Chairman Aer Rianta), Martin Dully (Chief Executive Aer Rianta).

*Photo – Aer Rianta Cork.*

the airport. The horrific air disaster had placed the airport at the centre of the aviation world news. The efficient handling of the tragic event was a credit to all concerned and drew great praise. The Airport General Manager, Barry Roche, expressed his deep appreciation of what had been done.

Among the very many messages of thanks received by airport management at Cork Airport, for the handling of a very tragic and complex disaster, were those from Jim Mitchell, T.D., Minister for Communications; Peter Barry, Minister for External Affairs; Joe Jennings, Head of Government Information Services; Kieran Doshi, Indian Ambassador to Ireland; C.D. Kolhe, Controller of Airworthiness, Government of India; Air India (UK); Dr. G.W., Middleton, Civilian Medical Officer with R.A.F.; Lieut. Commander R. G. Harrison, Royal Navy, Cornwall; Public Relations Office, Department of Defence, Whitehall, London; Joe Clark, Minister for External Affairs, Canada; The Editor, Toronto Star; The Canadian Broadcasting Corporation; Cardinal Lawrence T. Picahy, S.J. Roman Catholic Archbishop of Calcutta; Vincent H. Cruise, President Cork Chamber of Commerce and Denis Buckley, District Manager, Bord Telecom. Aer Rianta Chief Executive Martin Dully and Director Barra O Tuama expressed their appreciation of the great work done in connection with the disaster by all the services involved.

While Cork Airport returned to normal, the Royal Canadian Mounted Police, together with police agencies in Europe, India and Asia, continued the long and arduous investigations. Since the air disaster on 23rd June 1985 these investigations have revealed the following:

The black box recorded a thud, a muffled bang and a faint shriek. Fan blades on the engines were not bent indicating the engines were not running when the plane hit the water. Experts in the field of aviation from around the world came to the conclusion that more than likely, the air crash was caused by a bomb.

A further part of the ongoing investigation revealed that some days before the Air India disaster an unidentified male with a South East Asian accent telephoned Canadian Airlines international reservations desk in Vancouver and booked reservations on two flights after extensive enquiries with the reservations clerk. One of those flights was booked under the name of L. Singh who was to fly from Vancouver to Narita in Japan via Canadian airlines Flight 003 and on to Bangkok and Delhi via Air India on June 22nd. The other flight was booked under the name of M. Singh to fly from Vancouver to Toronto, Ontario, Canada. M. Singh was then to transfer to Air India Flight 182 en route to Delhi, India on 22nd June. A bearded Indian, male and wearing a mustard-coloured turban arrived at the ticket office and paid cash for the two bookings. Although the Singh luggage went on board both flights, neither of the two for whom the bookings were made, took the flights.

On the morning of June 23rd at 0713 G.M.T, a suitcase being unloaded from Canadian Airlines Flight 003 in Narita, Japan exploded killing two baggage handlers and injuring others. Approximately one hour later Flight 182 was blown from the skies. Resulting from the investigations, one of several suspects named Inderjit Singh Reyat was arrested, charged and convicted for his part in the Narita bomb explosion. He was sentenced to 10 years imprisonment. The Royal Canadian Mounted Police were convinced that the planning and organisation of the Air India disaster took place in Canada and the search went on for the perpetrators.

For the 1985 Air Spectacular at Cork, the French Air Force sent
two Alpha Jet trainers, one of which is seen here on the ground.
*Photo – Gabriel Desmond*

Three Irish Air Corps SIAI SF260W at Cork on 16th August 1985.
during rehearsal for the Air Spectacular.
*Photo – Gabriel Desmond.*

On 27th October 2000, the Royal Canadian Mounted Police arrested two men, believed to be connected with the Sikh extremist movement, responsible for the Air India disaster. They were Ajaib Singh Bagri and Ripudaman Singh Malik who were also accused of the 1985 bombing at Tokyo Narita Airport, which was intended to destroy another Air India flight with 177 people on board.

The authorities had long believed the explosion that destroyed the Air India Flight 182 and the other at Narita 54 minutes earlier, were the work of Sikh extremists waging a violent campaign against India for an independent homeland.

On 10th January 2001, a British Columbia Supreme Court Judge refused to release Malik and Bagri on bail. Police and media reports have said that at least five people were involved in the bombing plots. In October 2000, authorities had named two Canadian Sikh activists, Inderjit Singh Reyat and Talwinder Singh Palmer as indicted conspirators in the Air India attack. Palmer was killed by Indian police in 1992 and Reyat, as mentioned earlier, who was convicted of manslaughter for making the bomb that exploded at Narita Airport, is now in the final months of a ten-year sentence in a Canadian prison. This is the situation to date.

A memorial to the 325 people who died in the disaster was erected at Ahakista near Bantry, Co Cork and each year on the anniversary of the crash, relatives of the dead gather there to remember them.

## Airport's 25th Anniversary Celebrations

On 16th October 1986, Cork Airport celebrated its 25th anniversary with an 'open day'. It began with an EEC flag raising ceremony in the forecourt area by Peter Barry, T.D.,

A de Havilland DH84 Dragon painted as EI-ABI,"Iolar" the first plane of the
Aer Lingus fleet of 1936. On Open Day at Cork Airport 16th October 1986,
it flew the Lord Mayor and other guests on graceful circuits of the city.
*Photo – Gabriel Desmond*

A Colt hot air balloon was tethered beside the approach road during
Cork Airport Open Day.
*Photo – Gabriel Desmond*

Minister for Foreign Affairs. Also present were Frank Boland, Chairman of Aer Rianta; Martin Dully, Chief Executive Aer Rianta; Barry Roche, General Manager, Cork Airport and other senior executives of the Company. Also present were Brig. Gen. Connolly, G.O.C. Southern Command and Brig. Gen. McMahon, O.I.C. Air Corps. Following the opening, some spectacular flying events took place including aerobatics by pilot Paul Bonham and displays by the Air Corps, which included parachute jumps. An Aer Lingus BAC 1-11 did a low overshoot and guests of Aer Lingus including the Lord Mayor and civic dignitaries were taken on pleasure flights in a DH84 Dragon, painted as EI-ABI, *Iolar*, the first plane in the Company's fleet in 1936. Iona Airways, as well as putting on pleasure flights, did a banner-tow flight over the city at midday with the message 'Happy 25th Birthday Cork Airport'. Capt. Fergus O'Connor of Irish Helicopters gave a superb display in the big Sikorsky S61, EI-BHO based in Cork on gas and oil rig supply duties.

Huge crowds flocked to the airport for the birthday celebrations and the various airport services, airlines, state services etc. all put on exhibitions and display stands in the terminal building and exhibition tent. Aer Lingus and Dan Air sponsored a souvenir programme, the proceeds of which went to the Cork Branch of the Irish Arthritis Foundation. The airport taxi drivers arranged the free transport of senior citizens to the airport for the celebrations and Harringtons, the airport Caterers, provided free refreshments for them. Airport Handling and Brymon Airways sponsored signs specially made by students of the Cork School of Art.

The weather was perfect for the 'open day' and additional catering facilities were laid on in the operatives' canteen in

25 Year Celebration 1986: - Back Row L to R:- Denis Maher, Billy O'Keeffe, Tom Kerrigan, Paddy Dempsey Jack Riordan Airport Engineer. Middle Row L to R:- Mick Healy, Jerry O'Brien, Tom Russell, Sean McSweeney, Donie Harris, John Millner, Denis McSweeney, Mick McAuliffe. Seated L to R:- Barry Roche Airport General Manager, Kevin Farrell, Martin Dully, Chief Executive Aer Rianta, Pat Gallagher.

*Photo – Courtesy Irish Examiner*

the maintenance block. A VIP buffet was provided in the General Manager's office and Murrays and Hertz car hire firms provided Aer Rianta with two complimentary mini buses for use that day.

It was a day to remember and one on which the airport staff were able to look back with pride. Those who had stood on the tarmac on that dull October day in 1961 and who, 25 years on had done the same thing, were able to sense in no small way the great advances and expansions made at the airport in a quarter of a century

To conclude the celebrations, a dinner dance was held at Jury's Hotel attended by over 400 guests, including Peter Barry, T.D. Minister for Foreign Affairs.

In the Airport's 25th Anniversary Souvenir Programme, Frank Boland, Chairman of the Board of Aer Rianta wrote:

"The Airport is now firmly established as the major gateway to the south west and it was particularly gratifying to me in my first year as Chairman to be able to announce earlier this year that Cork Airport had moved from loss into profit for the first time in its history, We are leaving no stone unturned in our endeavour in this regard and I am optimistic that the Airport has a very bright future, to the benefit of all in the region. Today, however, we celebrate 25 years of service and excellence and we look forward to many more milestones in the Airport's development and in the future."

Martin Dully, Chief Executive Aer Rianta, wrote for the Souvenir Programme:

"In its 25 years history, the Airport has become a vital part of the whole infrastructure of Cork and its hin-terland, offering top class facilities to visitors and

142

Cork Airport APFS Officers with their Question Time Trophies
L to R:- Niall Bermingham, Oliver Jordon, Tom Breathnac, Mick O'Reilly, Mick Staunton, Jackie Daly.

*Photo - Courtesy Donie Harris*

local interests alike. We in Aer Rianta will continue in our efforts to ensure that the Airport plays a significant role in the well being and development of the region and we know we can count on your support for our efforts. It is appropriate also that we thank our airline friends and the many other agencies that have contributed to Cork Airport development during the past 25 years. Today is a significant milestone for Barry Roche and his team, many of them at Cork Airport right from its humble beginnings in 1961. I join with them and with you in celebrating to day and I wish the Airport continued success in the future."

In a Cork Examiner interview on the airport's 25th Anniversary, the General Manager said:

"When I recall the early days of Cork Airport, I think of the autumn of 1961. At that stage, there was only an unfinished structure surrounded by a vast expanse of mud. One wondered how large passenger aircraft could operate in such conditions. However, the air of adventure, of stepping into the unknown, seemed to affect almost everybody on the site. This embryo building and 6,000 feet of concrete would soon become a very important part of Cork's future. Just how big a part nobody knew – air transport was, until then, automatically associated with Dublin and Shannon. Only in then last few years had the huge Boeing jets taken over from the much slower Constellation and Britannia type aircraft on the transatlantic routes. Commercial aviation was in a period of rapid change and improvement. Soon we would be part of that world. ... It seems strange at

His Lordship Most Rev. John Magee, the newly consecrated Bishop of Cloyne
signing the Visitor's Book on his arrival at Cork Airport in March 1987.
Seated with him is the retiring Bishop of Cloyne, Most Rev. John Ahern.
*Photo –Courtesy Ray Shanahan*

Liberty Stream Balcony viewing area.
*Photo – Aer Rianta Cork*

this stage, looking back to the early days when we had time to polish the fire tenders twice per day. The airport has grown considerably since then and employment has increased four fold."

- - -

In 1987, the accommodation in the Control Tower etc. was restructured.

Because of the altitude of Cork Airport, approximately 500 feet above sea level, adverse weather had been a problem in the early years for aircraft landings. Some unduly harsh criticisms were often heard and remarks such as "'Tis built in the wrong place" and "It should have been built at Midleton" etc. were trotted out without very much idea as to why it was built at Ballygarvan. Initially, when the location was decided, the aviation experts of the day felt that the technological advances continually being made in Navigation and Landing Aids would considerably offset that problem in due course. In this they were correct.

- - -

The late Paddy Bracken, Senior Air Traffic Controller at Cork Airport undertook a project in the early '80s entitled " A Study of Disruption to Operations at Cork Airport due to Adverse Weather" which covered the period 1963 to 1982. In this study, he probed the many aspects of weather, which affected the landing and taking off of aircraft, the resultant diversions and the effect all of this had on the airport, the airlines concerned and the travelling public.

"Undoubtedly, the major influences on weather at Cork Airport are its altitude (about 500 feet above Ordnance Datum) and its exposure to the moist Atlantic in southeast to southwest air streams. .... The phenomenon causing greatest difficulty at Cork is reduced visibility in fog and drizzle.

146

Presentation at Cork Airport to the 500,000 passenger J.J. Walsh, Munster Express, Waterford in October 1987. L to R:- Máirín Ahern, Kay Carroll, Joe O'Connor, Asst. Apt. Manager, J.J. Walsh, Miriam Walsh, Lilibeth Horne, Sean Power, Harvey Travel, Waterford.

*Photo – Aer Rianta Cork*

147

Unlike Dublin and Shannon, the reduced visibility at Cork is actually due to low cloud (Stratus). … It is difficult to quantify the costs associated with each diversion and cancellation. There is no definite pattern. The circumstances can be quite varied. An early morning disruption will create different problems to one in the late evenings or during the night. Size of aircraft and category of passenger (business, tourist, private) will largely determine the social consequences of hardship endured."

The study of figures over a twenty years period showed that cancellations and diversions expressed as a percentage of commercial landings were 4.65% in 1963 but were down to 2.48% in 1982. There were high levels of disruption due to bad weather from 1963 to 1970 but from then on there was a decrease. Precision and Surveillance Radar came on stream in 1970 and led to a big reduction in the diversion rate.

There was still much to be done. The Government approved proposals for an extension of 1000 feet to the main runway and also proposals for "improved visual and electronic navigational aids to upgrade the international standard of the runway and a new Instrument Landing System (ILS) at both ends." The Minister, Mr. Jim Mitchell, in announcing this said that the proposed investment would give rise to significant improvements in the levels of services and facilities at the Airport and in particular they would ensure that:

(a) Airlines currently suffering load restriction penalties on certain routes ex Cork would be able to operate with increased payloads.

Aer Rianta recipients of 25 year service awards photographed with their wives January 1988. L to R:- Brendan Lynch, John Drennan, Barry Cullinane, Jerry Gregan, Miah Keohane, D. D. O'Leary.

*Photo – Aer Rianta Cork*

Section of the large crowd at the launch of Michael Barry's book THE STORY OF CORK AIRPORT 15th June 1988.
*Photo – Aer Rianta Cork.*

(b) The existing diversion problem at Cork Airport would be significantly reduced.

(c) Operational safety margins at the airport would be increased.

(d) Additional local employment in the construction industry would be generated during the course of the project.

(e) Cork Airport would be in a position to fulfil its important role in the provision of reliable transport facilities for tourism and other interests.

(f) The capacity of the Airport to attract new industries to the Cork area would be greatly enhanced.

In 1986, two highly sophisticated Instrument Landing Systems (ILS), one serving each end of the main runway 17/35 were installed, giving Cork Airport the distinction of becoming the first airport in the state to provide common frequency dual switchable systems on one runway. This facility allowed either end of the runway, depending on weather conditions, to be used for aircraft instrument landing approaches. The choice of system was at the discretion of the Air Traffic Controller.

Work began on the runway extension in autumn 1987 and was opened by John Wilson, Minister for Tourism and Transport, on 5th July 1989. High Intensity Approach Lights and Centre Line Lighting were also installed. On completion, the rating of the Instrument Landing System (ILS) was raised to Category II and the overall project had a profound effect on the weather diversion rate. Also installed was a computerised Instrument Runway Visual Range Measurement System. Following the completion of the entire project, the diversion rate was brought down to an average of 0.5% per annum.

Ballypehane school girls look on as Minister of State for Tourism, Denis Lyons, T.D. buries their time capsule at the extension of Cork Airport's main runway in 1989. Holding umbrella over the Minister is Barry Roche, Airport General Manager. On the left of picture are Phyl Walsh and Geraldine O'Donoghue Aer Rianta.

*Photo – Aer Rianta Cork.*

The official opening of the 1000 feet extension of the main runway by John Wilson,T.D.
Minister for Transport (centre) on 5th July 1989.  Others L to R:-Denis Maher(Duty Manager),
Barry Roche (Airport General Manager), Stephanie Kenneally (Aer Rianta), Frank Boland (Chairman Aer Rianta),
Bernard Allen T.D. Lord Mayor, Denis Lyons T.D. (Minister of State), Micheal Murphy, (APFS)),
Lilibeth Horne & Veronica O'Callaghan (Aer Rianta) .

*Photo – Gabriel Desmond*

25 year service presentations were made by Dermot Keogh, Chief Executive
Aer Rianta second from left to electricians Noel Daly and John O'Leary
at Cork Airport 1992.  On left Joe O'Connor, Asst. Airport Manager and
on right Barry Roche, Airport General Manager.
*Photo – Aer Rianta Cork.*

King Karl Gustav of Sweden inspects an army guard of honour
at the end of his State visit to Ireland 9th April 1992.
*Photo – Gabriel Desmond*

The runway extension also enabled the airport to accommodate large wide body aircraft. The first of these, an Aer Lingus Boeing 747 arrived on 5th July from Dublin to mark the official opening of the extension. The airport General Manager, Barry Roche, made a special presentation to the Captain of the aircraft in honour of the occasion. Large crowds gathered to watch the Jumbo touch down on Runway 17.

Meanwhile, Phase 1 of the Terminal Development was completed in 1988. This involved the relocation of the bar on the first floor from its existing location to the south end of the passenger terminal, thus allowing the area vacated to be used for public viewing and as an extension to the restaurant seating area. The work provided the unique "Wild Geese Bar", distinguished by its local themes captured in stained glass and complemented by aviation motifs in ceiling and seating. This phase of the development also gave the airport an extended restaurant and ground floor storage space and was completed at a cost of £340,000.

While the 1985 study examined capacity requirements for the following ten years, a 1988 analysis looked to the end of the century when the projected passenger figures would be in excess of a million and a quarter. The architects' objective was to transform the terminal into a facility, capable of meeting the various and diverse needs of all users, passengers, non-travelling public, airlines and airport staff. This would be achieved by alterations to existing buildings and extensions.

- - -

In May 1989, Iona Airways began a pilot training school at Cork Airport and in September the European College of Aeronautics opened a similar establishment. They were very

Yvonne Whitley and Tomás O Beara (Aer Rianta) leading a Cork
Airport group in the Cork St. Patrick's Day Parade of 1989.
*Photo – Aer Rianta Cork*

At the opening of the
European College of
Aeronautics Cork
Airport
17th Sept. 1989. On
the left- is Seamus
Brennan,T.D. Minister
for Tourism
and Transport, cut-
ting the tape with Dr.
Austin Daragh
Chairman on
the right. Behind
them is Brendan
McGann, Managing
Director.
*Photo – Aer Rianta
Cork*

In 1998, Cora Gleeson seen presenting presented Lilibeth Horne, Cork Airport Commercial Manager, with an equestrian bronze to mark 10 years of the Airport's Sponsorship of Clonmel Races held on 1st Nov each year. Also in picture is Vera Hewitt Mayor of Clonmel, and Jerry Desmond.

*Photo –Healy Racing Photographers*

Dan Air pioneered the Cork – Gatwick route with the HS748 aircraft and later with BAC 1-11s. This BAC 1-11 photo was taken from the tower in the last week that they operated the route - March 1989.
*Photo –Gabriel Desmond*

Three budding "Ken Dohertys" in November 1989 APFS – Miah Keohane, Owen McSweeney, Jackie Daly.
*Photo – Aer Rianta Cork*

158

successful but a slowdown in requirement for pilots due to recession in the aviation industry caused both schools to close in 1992.

- - -

The passenger figures for the latter half of the decade showed considerable increase, the 1989 figure being 627,032.

In 1990, when Ireland held the E.U. Presidency, a meeting of European Foreign Ministers was held in Kenmare, Co. Kerry. This led to a large number of Government Jets visiting Cork from all over Europe.

Phase II of the expansion and development of the Terminal Building was completed in 1990. This included the creation of a spacious new baggage hall on the ground floor, the extension of the departure lounge, a temporary Duty Free Shop on the second floor and the provision of extra office space. The main ramp was extended northwards. This phase was officially opened by the Taoiseach, Charles J. Haughey, on 24th February 1991. He also inaugurated a new Access Control Security System.

## Light Aircraft crash near Bandon (1992).

Two single engined light aircraft collided in mid air in the Bandon area on the afternoon of 26th February 1992. The aircraft were on a training flight and were operated by Iona Airways, who ran a Pilot Training School at Cork Airport. One of the planes was able to return to the airport, the other, a Cessna 172, crashed at Knocknagallagh, 3 miles on the Clonakilty side of Bandon. Both occupants, Seamus Campbell and James Kennedy were killed.

- - -

Phase III of the work was completed in 1992. It provided the airport with a magnificent new Duty Free Shop, almost

Barry Roche (Airport General Manager) making a presentation to the Captain of the Aer Lingus Boeing 747 which flew in for the official opening of the extension to the main runway 5th Jul y 1989.  It was Cork's first 747 and the largest aircraft ever to land at the airport.
*Photo – Gabriel Desmond*

Cork Airport Taxi Driver of the year award 1990.
Peter Kearney (Winner), Denis Lyons T.D. Minister of State, Phyl  Walsh Lilibeth Horne, Michael Staunton, Denis Maher.
*Photo – Aer Rianta Cork*

doubled in size. It did business of over £3 million in its first year – the first time that Cork exceeded that sum. It was officially opened by Maire Geoghegan Quinn, Minister for Tourism and Transport, on 23rd July '92. In her speech, she described Aer Rianta as "one of the jewels in the State's Crown" of semi-State Companies. She referred to their superb work both at home and abroad and as just one example, Cork Airport's very attractive new Duty Free facility.

Phase III also provided further enhancement of the public concourse. The airport got its third departure gate, a new Departures Lounge, Arrivals Hall and a new Customs Channel and Friskem. Extra State Services offices were also provided, together with an open plan Information Centre, which included a Customer Service Desk and a Customer Service Car Park Desk. The Bank of Ireland was given a new location and included a Bureau de Change. Celtic floor patterns were used extensively. Disembarked passengers stepped into the Arrivals Hall, with information screens in several languages, to experience the warm glow from an open fire. While waiting for their luggage to be delivered on the carousel, two beautiful granite water features gave a restful appearance. Fish aquariums also added to the scene. This phase also included the provision of a Boardroom/Conference Room, known as the Orchard Room. Bewleys Café was also opened under Phase III on the 8th January 1992.

Phase IV of the Passenger Terminal Development was officially opened by Brian Cowan, Minister for Transport, Energy and Communications, on 26th October 1994. Attending also were Noel Hanlon, Chairman Aer Rianta, Derek Keogh, Chief Executive of the Company, the Lord Mayor,Tom Falvey and the Lady Mayoress. This phase of the

The crowded terminal on Open Day, St. Patrick's Day 1992.
*Photo – Gabriel Desmond*

Former News Editor of the Cork Examiner (now Irish Examiner), Stephen Coughlan, to his surprise had a new room at Cork Airport named in his honour in 1993. He is pictured here unveiling a plaque bearing his name. Also present George Crosbie of the Cork Examiner and Barry Roche. Airport General Manager.

*Photo – John Sheehan Photography*

163

His Excellency Pres. Mario Soares of Portugal inspecting a Guard of Honour at Cork Airport prior to his departure on 4th June 1993 following a State visit.
*Photo –Courtesy Irish Examiner*

development was the largest of the four phases. It provided new airline and car hire desks, new ticket desks, and an enlarged departure area. It also provided a completely new Vertical Circulation Area (VCA), an escalator and two panoramic lifts. The use of natural materials i.e. granite, marble, water and light was continued from the previous phase with the inclusion of a further two water features with granite and marble enclosures – one at the base of the lifts and the other adjacent to the check-in desks. Glass was used to enclose the Vertical Circulation Area with its stairs and glazed panoramic lifts. In the main entrance area, a sculpture of Christy Ring, the famous Cork hurler was located as was a fish-pond and sculpture of Jack Charlton, former Irish Soccer Manager. The Celtic floor patterns, extensively used in Phase III were continued in Phase IV in front of the check-in desks and around the departure floor. The Celtic patterns were cut into the natural linoleum floor covering used in all the phases.

Phases I - IV of the development and expansion of the terminal cost £8.2 million. The airport had been opened in 1961 with a total floor terminal area of 3,400 square metres. An additional floor area of 400 square metres was added in 1976. The four phases added between 1988 and 1994 gave an additional 8,300 square metres making a total floor area of 12,100 square metres with a projected capacity of 1 million passengers in the year 2000. In fact, by the end of 1996, the passenger figures at Cork Airport had reached one million.

To meet increasing demands, a new Freight Terminal was needed. Work began on the one million pounds project in April 1994 and it became operational in November 1995. The old freight building, now called Compass House, was later remodelled to accommodate Aer Lingus Engineering and

President Chiluba of Zambia bidding farewell to President Mary Robinson and the Lord Mayor of Cork Joe O'Callaghan at Cork Airport 18th Nov. 1995 before boarding his flight to London following his Sate visit.

*Photo – Aer Rianta Cork*

Loading staff. It also gave office space for Aer Lingus Sales Dept.

Two new freight buildings, were completed in May 1998. The freights companies use their own aircraft for overnight freight to and from the airport. The North Ramp project, which consisted of an extension of that ramp, the laying of a new apron and taxiway and the widening of existing taxiway "Delta" became operational in 1998.

- - -

In March 1998, Barry Roche retired as Airport General Manager. His was the longest tenure of all of Cork Airport's Managers (1984-1998) and it was the period of greatest change and development in the airport's history.

The early eighties was a time of economic stagnation and Cork Airport was in a loss-making environment with little prospect of investment or development. Barry Roche led a twin-track initiative - to reduce costs and to grow traffic. In a few years the success of this strategy began to manifest itself. A £1 million marketing project, led to significant passenger traffic growth of 87% between 1984 and 1989. Profitability was achieved and investment quickly followed. The main runway, 17/35, was extended by 1,000 ft. and centre line lighting was installed, This facilitated the introduction of Category 2 Instrument Landing Systems which had a huge effect in reducing the diversion rate from 4% to 0.2% in the first year of its operation. The airside improvements were followed by a major Terminal Building extension that was completed in 1994. The new terminal, with a capacity of 1.1 million passengers, had many unique features, which reflected Barry Roche's desire to have a building with 'character' as well as functionality. The central water feature in the main concourse, the welcoming open fire in Arrivals, and sculp-

A group of 40 Piper Comanche owners converged on Cork in May 1996 from as far away as the US, Sweden and Israel.
*Photo – Gabriel Desmond*

tures of his heroes Christy Ring and Jack Charlton, are all testament to his imaginative approach in helping passengers feel relaxed in what might otherwise be a stressful environment.

Barry's determination to achieve targets, which his unique foresight identified, marked him as a special person. He had come up through the ranks, having started work as a Police/Fireman when Cork Airport opened in 1961, He believed in communication at all levels and he showed by example, that any goal can be attained with application and determination.

Barry Roche set a fine example for young aspiring employees that opportunities are there for the taking and that any hill can be climbed. He retired in 1998 and lives in his beloved native Cork City.

- - -

Observations of the main runway 17/35 made over recent years showed a gradual but significant deterioration in the condition of the concrete surface. This, together with the loading imposed by modern aircraft and the age of the runway, which had been laid in 1960/61, indicated that it was approaching the end of its useful life. It was imperative, therefore, that remedial works be carried out. To restore the runway surface and extend its life span for a further 10 years, it was decided to cover the runway with an asphalt overlay 150 mm thick. The width of the runway was 45 metres (Code Letter D) and to meet current specifications of 60 metres for that Code, it was necessary to construct shoulders of 7.5 metres wide on each side. The shoulders consisted of a granular base course on which was placed a surface of Marshall Asphalt 100 mm thick. The work, which commenced in November 1998 and completed in May 1999 was carried out

A hard-working Santa Claus in 1997 enters into the spirit of Christmas, that is always created by Aer Rianta for passengers, visitors and especially for children at Xmas time. Extreme right is APF P. J. Cahalane.

*Photo –Courtesy Ray Shanahan*

at night, causing the least inconvenience to traffic. In the operation, the existing runway edge lights were replaced. Also, before the overlay construction, it was necessary to remove the runway centreline and touchdown zone lights and reinstall them on completion of the overlay.

By the end of 1999 passenger traffic had reached 1,501,805.

- - -

Towards the end of 2000, Electrical Engineer Jack McGrath retired. When he first arrived in Cork Airport in January 1961, the runways were still under construction and the Control Tower had yet to be built. He had been transferred from Dublin to head up the Aviation Radio Section of the Post Office Engineering Branch (POED) and subsequently crossed over from the Post Office to the Dept. of Transport and Power. He was responsible for the embryonic Aviation Radio Service at Cork Airport, which was the forerunner of the present Engineering Division of the Air Navigation Service.

When Mt Gabriel Secondary Surveillance Radar (SSR) station was set up he was the Irish representative in the European consortium charged with the choosing of the site and the construction of the radar base. Based at the airport since 1961, he was involved in the development of the National Maritime Radio Network and played a pivotal role in the setting up of the Irish Marine Emergency Service, which comprises 52 stations around the country providing state of the art communications from Malin to Mizen and all points between.

When the oil tanker Betelgeuse blew up in Bantry Bay in 1979, Cork Airport became the focal point of the rescue and subsequent investigation and Jack used his considerable engineering knowledge and expertise to set up a closed cir-

President Yoweri Kaguta Musevani of Uganda signing the Visitors Book
at Cork Airport  November 2000 watched by (left) Joe O'Connor, Airport
Gen. Manager and Micheal Martin, T.D. Minister for Health.
*Photo – News Pic's Press Photo Agency Ltd.*

Jack McGrath B.E. Irish Marine Emergency Service (now Irish Coast Guard)
pictured at Cork Airport on his retirement October 2000. At rear
L to R:-Martin Ryan, Cait Ward, Ann Walsh, Willie O'Connor.
*Photo – Courtesy Cait Ward*

cuit TV Centre and converted a ballroom into a series of sound proof simultaneous translation booths. For his efforts in this regard he received a commendation from the then Attorney General, Declan Costello.

On his retirement Jack McGrath held the post as Chief Engineer of the Irish Marine Emergency Service (now the Irish Coast Guard).

The Christy Ring Sculpture on the ground floor of the terminal
at Cork Airport.
*Photo – Courtesy Irish Examiner*

# 5

# CHAPTER FIVE

As mentioned in chapter three, Cork Airport opened in 1961 under the control of and management by the Department of Transport and Power. That situation remained until 1968 when management functions were transferred to Aer Rianta. The functions of Aer Rianta cpt, which is a public limited company, came about as follows.

The Air Navigation and Transport Act 1936 empowered the then Minister for Industry and Commerce (predecessor to the present Minister for Public Enterprise) to establish and maintain airports as part of the framework for the development of civil aviation in Ireland. It also provided for the formation of a limited company to serve as a holding company for Aer Lingus/Aerlinte – the Irish National Airlines. Aer Rianta cpt was established in 1937 in pursuance of this provision. It was not until the Air Navigation and Transport Act 1946 that Aer Rianta was actually named as the Company.

Scheduled air services commenced from Dublin Airport in 1940. Between 1940 and 1950 Aer Rianta managed Dublin Airport as agent of the then Minister for Industry and Commerce. In 1950, statutory responsibility for the management of Dublin Airport as agent of the Minister was given to Aer Rianta by virtue of Section 23 of the Air Navigation and Transport Act 1950. Scheduled services from Shannon Airport commenced in 1945 under the management of the Department of Industry and Commerce and its successor the

Department of Transport and Power (now the Department of Public Enterprise). Cork Airport operated in the same fashion when it opened in 1961.

In 1966, in pursuance of the requirements of the Air Companies Act 1966, Aer Rianta's shareholding in Aer Lingus/Aer Linte was transferred to the Minister for Finance and as a result, Aer Rianta's sole function became the management of Dublin Airport as agent of the Minister. In 1969, the management of both Shannon and Cork Airports was transferred on the basis of an administrative arrangement to Aer Rianta, thus giving Aer Rianta responsibility for the management of the three State airports.

Aer Rianta has operated as a Commercial State body since 1969 despite the agency arrangement and notwithstanding the fact that the company did not own the airports assets nor had it underpinning legislation put in place. Since 1986 the company has funded all new capital developments at the three airports at a total cost of about £240 million.

It was always the Government's intention to establish Aer Rianta as a statutory airports' authority and consideration was given in the intervening years to the preparation of necessary legislation. However, the proposal was deferred over the years since, owing to the serious downturn of tourism and the effect of this on airport revenues, the prospects of sustaining an integrated airports authority and of funding the airport capital development programme otherwise than from the Exchequer were not good. In the event, the legislation did not come into being until 1998 when the Air Navigation and Transport (Amendment) Act 1998 was passed into law on 5th July 1998.

Under that Act, ownership of the assets of the three airports was transferred to Aer Rianta on Vesting Day, 1st

Aer Rianta Conference Room at Cork Airport.
*Photo – Aer Rianta Cork*

January 1999. A range of other powers, previously held by the Minister in relation to the operation of airports, were also transferred. These included power to execute leases/licence, power to acquire land compulsorily, make bye-laws and appoint authorised persons to enforce them and also to carry out certain functions relating to the operation and management of the airport. For the first time, the company has the statutory power to dispose of abandoned aircraft.

## Aer Rianta Cork.

The smooth operation of the airport is centred around the functions of Aer Rianta Management on the one hand and those of the airlines, State, Semi-State and ancillary services on the other. This is not apparent on the surface and it is only when some major incident occurs, such as the Air India Disaster in 1985, that one sees how vitally important the proper functioning of all those services is. Passengers through the airport invariably deal with airport police, airline officials and customs officers. What goes on behind the scenes to enable the airport function smoothly is not obvious.

The General Manager of Cork Airport is Joe O'Connor. A native of Blarney, he was appointed to his present position in March 1998, having spent 12 years as Assistant Manager. He had worked as a Duty Manager for most of his airport career, which commenced in 1966 when he joined the Civil Service. The Assistant General Manager is Sheila Murphy.

Aer Rianta functions are carried out by a variety of Departments such as Administration, Commercial, Marketing, Engineering/Maintenance, Airport Police/Fire Service Operations etc.

Other Aer Rianta Departments include Purchasing, Property and Information Technology managed by Tomás Ó

The V.I.P. Lounge at Cork Airport on completion of Phase II of the Expansion and Development Plan in 1990.

*Photo – Aer Rianta Cork*

Thirsty airport staff punters at Fir Grove Hotel, Mitchelstown en route from Clonmel Races 1995.
Standing L to R: Bernie Spillane, Joe Hennessy, Yvonne Foley, Jerry O'Donnell, Seamus Moriarty.
Seated L to R:- Phyl Walsh, Roger Maloney, Sean McSweeney, Mick Staunton,
Terence O'Connor, Liam Ryan, Mick Ward.
*Photo – Aer Rianta Cork*

Béara. Training is under the control of Regina Collins O'Neill, Finance under Finance Manager Eddie Fitzgibbon and Michael Beasley runs the Car Parks.

The role of Aer Rianta has changed dramatically in recent years. Issues such as safety and security are highly regulated and much more formalised than heretofore. Cork Airport now requires to be licensed by the Irish Aviation Authority under the Irish Aviation Authority (1993) Act as amended by the Aer Rianta (1998) Act. Licensing conditions impose onerous responsibilities on Aer Rianta to ensure that operational standards are maintained.

The Aviation Regulation Bill, which was enacted recently, gives extensive powers to the Commission for Aviation Regulation and ensures that airport charges are transparent and non-discriminatory. This takes the issue of airport charges out of the political arena and ensures that airlines and customers get reasonable value for money.

Airport Management is currently engaged in upgrading all systems with the best available modern technology. This ensures that efficiency and high standards are maintained despite the pressures of a rapidly expanding business.

In an era when all aspects of business are going through transformations including airlines and traditional state services, it is still the key objective of Aer Rianta to deliver the best possible service to airport users in a customer friendly style. Thankfully, this tradition has not been lost by the present generation of airport workers.

The Duty Managers represent the General Manager on a shift basis and are responsible for the airport's day-to-day activities; they also oversee the Operations Office, Switchboard and Customer Service Desk on the ground floor

A delighted Joe Hoare from Douglas Cork with champagne in hand,
was the millionth passenger to pass through Cork Airport in Nov. 1997.
L to R:- Máirín Ahern (Marketing), Frank Walsh (Servisair), Joe Hoare, Lilibeth Horne (Commercial Manager), Barry Roche (Apt. Gen. Manager), Dearnbhla O'Brien (Marketing Manager Ryanair), Alan Long (Servisair Manager).

*John Sheehan Photography*

182

and deal with the other airport services, co-ordinating their activities where necessary.

## Commercial Operations.

The airport obtains its revenue both from aviation and non-aviation ventures. Passenger traffic is a major source of income due to the load fee per person charged. This fee is built into the cost of each airline ticket and at present is £4.00 for internal flights, £7.23 European flights and £9.04 on transatlantic flights. The greater the passenger traffic, the greater that source of revenue.

Over the forty years operations at the airport, there have been only a few occasions when the annual passenger figures didn't show an increase. These situations have already been dealt with in a previous chapter. However, it wasn't until 1986 that passenger traffic began to show a vast improvement and since then, Cork Airport hasn't looked back. By the end of 1996, passenger numbers had risen to almost 1.125 million and at the end of 1999 well over one and a half million passengers had used the airport. The huge increase in numbers boosted considerably the passenger load fees.

A considerable portion of the airport's income is derived from car parking, rent of office space and concessions such as car hire desks, freight, catering and banking facilities etc. Another source of revenue for the airport is obtained from aircraft landing fees and parking. It costs £347.44 to land an A321 series 200 airbus, as used by Aer Lingus on its London routes and £48.16 for a 3 to 24 hours parking, should that be necessary.

Of greatest significance with regard to revenue for the airport was the Duty Free and Tax Free Shops, the former alas now very much curtailed. Prior to 1978, the duty free facility did not apply to passengers travelling to the UK, only to Europe. There was a revision of legislation in 1977/78, which permitted duty free sales to passengers travelling to the UK. Aer Rianta then opened its own Duty Free Shop at Cork Airport for liquor and opened a Tax Free shop in February 1979. The shops were enlarged in 1983 and refurbished in 1986.

From the mid '80s onwards, the Duty Free business at Cork flourished in line with unprecedented traffic growth. 1998, which was the last full year of Duty Free shopping, generated £3.5 million profit. On the 30th June 1999, following an unsuccessful bid to retain duty free sales throughout Europe, abolition took place.

Aer Rianta retained Duty Free sales outside of the EU and is building a new retail business called Travel Value for shopping within the union. Travel Value offers passengers travelling within the EU savings of up to 25% on crystal, cosmetics and perfume. New, exciting and innovative products will be sought to make future shopping at Irish Airports a worthwhile and interesting experience.

Of the three Aer Rianta owned airports, Cork suffered most because of the abolition of Duty Free. Cork Airport traffic is 95% inter EU and only 5% outside of the union. Duty Free was a licence to print money and that licence was revoked. The airport will never generate the same profits as before but it still will have a viable and lucrative retail business.

In November 2000, Cork Airport opened a new look Travel Value shop. Barriers to entry were removed and a new frontage with Travel Value branding was put in place. A customised cosmetic area and revamped perfume bays create

In Nov. 1997 at Clonmel Races sponsored by Aer Rianta Cork, when Gas-a-Tina, won the last race. L to R:- Ruby Walsh (Jockey), Colon O'Leary (Aer Rianta), Maureen Mullins (wife of trainer), Arthur Dinan (Owner), John Smyth (Marketing Manager Cork Airport),Donna McSweeney (Aer Rianta), Paddy Mullins (Trainer).

*Photo – Healy Racing Photographers*

a Fragrance Boutique. A new and delightfully appointed crystal area attracts traffic from the departure area. New flooring and relocation of the existing department combine to offer passengers convenient and value shopping at the new Travel Retail shop while still retaining Duty Free for passengers travelling outside the EU. The Commercial Manager at Cork Airport is Lilibeth Horne.

## Marketing

Although passenger numbers through Cork Airport always exceeded expectations, local management felt there was a need to dedicate a special effort to developing new business for the airport. This was quite a new concept in the 1970s, whereas nowadays almost every airport has a Marketing Department.

The first pioneer in the role of 'Commercial Development Superintendent' for Cork Airport was Barry Roche, who was appointed to the position in 1974. He succeeded in forging strong links in the UK, which resulted in the addition of services from Cardiff and Bristol with Dan Air in the mid-1970s and a service from Plymouth to Cork in 1976. Dan Air subsequently introduced a summer service from Cork to Jersey. Plymouth may not have seemed the most obvious route at the time. It was operated by Brymon Airways originally, using a Cessna Skymaster and subsequently an 18-seater Twin Otter. It proved to be a very successful niche market, which has gone from strength to strength over the years and today the Plymouth service runs 6 times a week using a sophisticated 50-seater Dash-8.

At this time there were also many opportunities to develop inbound traffic from the Continent, both on charter and

At launch of Brymon fly/train product Autumn 1984. L to R:- Barry Roche, Airport Gen. Manager; Tom Haughey, Marketing; John Jones, Sales Manager Brymon Airways.

*Photo – Aer Rianta Marketing*

At commencement of Air France summer schedule 1987.
L to R:- Pierce Wagner, Air France Manager Ireland; Máirín Ahern, Promotions Officer – Europe; Declan Meagher, Air France Sales Manager; George Barter, T. Barter International.
*Photo – Aer Rianta Marketing*

the scheduled services from Paris and Amsterdam. Barry Roche recruited Máirín Meany as Promotions Assistant in 1978. However, it was still felt that Cork was at a disadvantage due to its limited promotions budget. Aer Rianta, led by Chief Executive Martin Dully and Barry Roche, took a major initiative in 1984 with the setting up of "CORK AIRPORT MARKETING", a new entity with a budget of £1 million and the target of producing an annual passenger throughput of 400,000 within 5 years. How ambitious that seemed at the time! Total passenger traffic through Cork in 1984 was around 333,000. Annual growth was less than 5% as this was a period of economic gloom with high national unemployment levels, while in Cork City there was the closure of major employers such as Ford Motors, Dunlops, Ranks, etc.

Tom Haughey was recruited from Shannon Development to head up the new organisation, which operated from down-town offices in the South Mall.     This boosted the airport profile of Cork Airport in the city. The first 'statement of intent' was the new slogan "Cork Airport is Taking Off!" which though launched in times of depression became something of a rallying cry when the airport demonstrated continuing growth.

An extensive base of contacts was developed, including Airlines, outbound tour operators such as JWT and Blueskies and overseas tour operators in the main markets of continental Europe.   They marketed Cork as a tourist destination at the major Trade Fairs in France, Benelux, Germany, Switzerland and Scandinavia with the result that the people specialising in selling Ireland in those markets included Cork in their planning.  Tom also saw the benefit of consolidating business on existing routes and many exciting promotions came into being such as "Love is in the Air", a radio competition centred around St Valentine's Day to boost travel to London at a quiet time of the year. Another 'ground breaker' at the time was the introduction of the concept of a "Sky + Rail" combination. In those pre-competition days, air travel between Ireland and London was very expensive, costing anything from £120 to £240 for a return flight from Cork to London. Cork Airport Marketing got together with the marketing people from Brymon Airways and came up with a product costing just £89, which offered a return flight from Cork to Plymouth, taxi transfer to the railway station and a train connection to London! This amazing idea actually worked and the fact that the 'psychological barrier' of £100 was undercut resulted in a lot of positive press coverage. British Rail were so pleased with the extra exposure they got from it that they went on to improve the product by offering rail connections from Plymouth to other accessible points such as Swindon and Reading and the whole idea began to attract people who would have travelled to these areas via Heathrow. Another exciting 'first' for Cork Airport during this time was the first non-stop commercial charter flight to the USA, a B707 operated by Buffalo Air to Philadelphia. It was newsworthy because the possibilities for even medium haul destinations were very limited at the time as the length of the main runway was only 6000 ft.

The 6000 ft runway had in fact always been an impediment to traffic growth as there were load penalties on even relatively close holiday destinations such as Rimini and Palma, which resulted in higher charges for people to fly from Cork. In 1985 Cork Airport Marketing secured a winter charter series to Gran Canaria which had to operate outward via Shannon each week on the outbound leg as Cork did not have sufficient runway length. This was important because it

John K. Smyth, Aer Rianta Marketing Manager, makes a presentation to Captain Ed.Rogero of Rich Airlines on the inaugural flight to Orlando, Florida on 16th June 1996. Left is Denis Maher, Duty Manager and on right is John Prendergast, agent for Rich International.

*Photo – Gabriel Desmond*

subsequently helped to make a case for extending Cork's runway by an extra 1000 ft.

In the autumn of 1986 Mairín Meany invited TV chef Keith Floyd to visit the Kinsale gourmet festival in an attempt to promote the Plymouth connection. At the time he had only had limited exposure in the UK and none in Ireland but having been assured that he was 'something different' and fond of an occasional glass of wine it was felt he might add to the festivities. As soon as he saw the quay in front of Actons Hotel with sun shining, tide in, swans and sailing boats he was enraptured and declared he must do a TV programme here! There followed an amount of work convincing his producer, the BBC and undertaking a lot of research into real and imagined links between Cork and the West Country. A year later two half-hour length programmes had been made using material from all over County Cork and broadcast in two different series on BBC nationwide. This was where Darina Allen made her TV debut!   Keith became very attached to Kinsale and ended up buying a house there, which he lived in, when his busy schedule permitted, for about 10 years.

By the 4th year of operation the marketing unit had surpassed its targets.  Tom Haughey moved on to a new role at Aer Rianta Head Office and the marketing function reverted to the airport.   From 1988 to 1995 the marketing team of Máirín Ahern and Lilibeth Horne continued the task of developing new routes and promoting the existing ones through vigorous advertising and PR campaigns. During this time the airport had scheduled services with Aer Lingus, British Airways, Air France, KLM, Ryanair, CityFlyer, Brymon Airways, Brit Air, to name but a few. There was a significant increase in incoming charter series from France, Switzerland, Scandinavia, Benelux and Iceland and, most importantly, after the runway extension was completed in 1989 the range of sun destinations began to improve dramatically, offering Cork people direct access to such places as Tunisia, the Canary Islands, Greece, Cyprus, Turkey and even Florida. There was even a mini charter series from New York in the summer of 1991, operated by Sceptre Tours using American Trans Air B 757 aircraft. In addition, some specialist Ski operators began to introduce direct winter departures from Cork to Austria, France (for Andorra) and Italy.

By 1994 Cork Airport's traditional catchment area of Cork and Kerry had grown to include Waterford, Tipperary, Kilkenny and South Limerick due to successful press and radio advertising campaigns as well as high-profile sponsorship of events such as Clonmel Races and Millstreet Horse Show. The attraction for Munster people in flying out of Cork was easy accessibility, no congestion, cheap car parking and a customer-friendly terminal with relaxing water features and tasteful works of art.

In April 1995 John Smyth joined Aer Rianta as Marketing Manager at Cork Airport. He had previously been Sales Manager – Southern Europe for Aer Lingus based in Paris and had a vast amount of experience and contacts in the airline business. He brought a new focus to the marketing strategy. He introduced Cork Airport to the Internet, unheard of at the time. Traffic continued to increase rapidly and in November, 1996 the millionth passenger in a year passed through Cork Airport for the first time.

The summer of 1998 was to be a major turning point in the development of services out of Cork Airport as after months of negotiations, Aer Lingus extended their direct Amsterdam service to a daily year-round operation, while the same happened on the Paris route the following year. The Aer Lingus

Wedding presentation to Tom Pyke (Electrical) by Airport Maintenance Staff on 17th Sept, 1991. Back Row L to R:- Brendan Lynch, Bob Donovan, Tony Deenihan, Robt. Allan, John Mulcahy. Front Row L to R:- John O'Leary, Mary Murphy, George Green, Jack Riordan Airport Engineer, Tom Pyke, Paddy Collins, Joe Maguire, John Drennan, Billy Lawlor, Tim Murphy, Sean Staunton.

*Photo – Aer Rianta Cork*

194

presence has continued to grow at Cork Airport to the point where they now overnight up to 4 aircraft there and employ in excess of 150 people. The Amsterdam service was doubled to twice daily in the Summer and the benefits of Aer Lingus' involvement in the One World Alliance are being also exploited. Boeing 737–800s and Airbus 321s are now daily visitors to Cork Airport. Traffic grew from 1.1 million passengers in 1996 to 1.7 million in 2000. The Marketing Department, now boosted with the addition of Louise O'Connor and Liz O'Sullivan, has just secured a new holiday series to Elat in Israel. This year, Cork Airport has 10 airlines serving 16 scheduled routes, as well as 36 flights per week to 17 holiday destinations. If any further evidence of confidence is required, the fact that a new 3 million capacity terminal is being planned is proof that the talented marketing efforts of Cork Airport have been singularly successful.

Thanks to Martin Dully (RIP), Barry Roche, Tom Haughey, Máirín Ahern, Lilibeth Horne, John Smyth, Louise O'Connor and Liz O'Sullivan as well as many others such as Joe O'Reilly and Charlie Cullinane, '**Cork Airport is Taking Off.**'

# Engineering/Maintenance.

The Engineering and Maintenance section of Aer Rianta is responsible for the airfield and landside maintenance as well as being involved in airport planning and development. A considerable amount of maintenance is necessary to keep the airport buildings, runways and taxiways and the many acres of land up to specific standards. All of this is the responsibility of the Operations and Facilities Manager Bill Daly and his maintenance staff under foreman Tony Deenihan.

The electrical, fitter and plumbing sections at the airport also come under Engineering/Maintenance. George Greene

Retirement presentation to Barry Cullinane, Aer Rianta Maintenance July 1991

Back Row L to R:- Brendan Lynch, Joe Maguire, Paddy Hurley, John Mulcahy, Bobby Donovan, Mick Beasley.

Middle Row L to R:- John O'Leary, Paddy Collins, Billy Lawlor, Robert Allen, Tony Deenihan, Johnny Flavin, John Drennan, George Green, Joe O'Connor, Asst. Airport Manager,

Front Row L to R: Jack Riordan, Airport Engineer, Barry Cullinane, Mrs Mary Cullinane, Mary Murphy.

*Photo – Aer Rianta Cork*

Retirement presentation by maintenance staff for Jack Riordan, Cork Airport Engineer, 31st July 1994. L to R:- Joe Maguire, Tom Pyke, Mary Murphy, John McSweeney, Billy O'Keeffe, Noel Daly, Tony Deenihan, Jack Riordan, John Drennan, Mrs. Siobhan Riordan, Johnny Flavin, Bob Donovan, George Green.

*Photo – Aer Rianta Cork*

heads the staff of electricians responsible for supplying power to all services and buildings at the airport. There are responsible for runway, taxiway, approach and obstruction lighting, operation and maintenance of the airport's standby generators, automatic car park barriers, electronic-opening doors and electrical maintenance of the airport vehicles.

Joe Maguire is the resident fitter and he maintains all mechanically operated equipment. Airport plumbing which includes water, sewerage and central heating is the responsibility of Robert Allen whose father Sam Allen was the airport plumber from early days until his retirement. The central heating for the terminal is supplied from gas boilers.

Health and safety is also the responsibility of the Operations and Facilities Manager. Daily and weekly reports are compiled and analysed by both the local safety committee and corporate safety manager. Items are addressed efficiently. These reports are co-ordinated by Seamus Aherne, Engineering Administration.

The current members of the Aer Rianta Safety Committee at Cork Airport are Marc Lake (APFS), Tom O'Neill (Maintenance), Fergal Gearty (Clerical) and Wendy Sheehan (Commercial).

Tom Fitzgerald has been resident Clerk of Works at Cork Airport for the past decade, overseeing various contract projects.

# Airport Police and Fire Service.

Passengers' safety and security is of paramount importance to Aer Rianta and the Airport Police/Fire Service play a vital role to ensure this. The official with overall responsibility for the Service at Cork Airport is Chief Airport Security Officer

At the passing out of new recruits to the Airport Police/FireService in May 1997. Back Row L to R:-APFs Eoghan Calnan, Anthony Healy, James Kelly, Trevor Healy, Trevor O'Connor, S.McSuibhne, Marc Lake, Kevin. Dunne, Kieran O'Regan, Declan Healy. Front Row L to R:- AFOs Mick Staunton, Pat Gallagher and Ger. Harvey; Barry Roche (Apt. Gen. Manager), Michael Healy (CASO), AFOs Arthur O'Leary & Denis. McSweeney.

*Photo -Aer Rianta Cork.*

(C.A.S.O.) Michael Healy. It is provided as a necessary unit to the operational needs of the airport. Both elements, Police and Fire Service are there to ensure the safety of passengers. At Dublin, Shannon and Cork, the Airport Police and Fire Services are provided by the one unit. This is a unique situation and is particular to this country.

All safety considerations for air transport i.e. physical facilities, type of services, conditions of operation, passenger facilities, etc. are regulated through I.C.A.O. (International Civil Aviation Organisation). This body exists as an extension of the United Nations Organisation dealing specifically with air transport. By agreement, it lays down regulations for the running of the air transport industry internationally. Aer Rianta, as an Irish semi-state agent, operates, on behalf of the Department of Public Enterprise, the 3 main airports (Dublin, Shannon and Cork) within the framework of l.C.A.O.

The original recruitment to the Police/Fire Service at Cork Airport in 1961 was to have been eleven Wardens, as they were then called. This was increased to twenty-two within two years. Over the following years, staff numbers increased slowly in twos and threes, culminating in 1979 with an intake of 14 which brought the total then in the force to 52. The large intake of staff was due mainly to the political unrest in the country at that time, caused by the situation in Northern Ireland.

A further eighteen years passed before recruitment again took place in 1997. Due to natural causes, numbers had dwindled and as a result ten new young recruits took up duty in May of that year. The airport now was vibrant with passenger throughput numbers increasing by up to 15% annually. As a result, it was decided in 1998 to make the airport operational on a 24-hour basis. Further recruitment

Passing out photograph of new recruits to the Airport Police/Fire Service in August 1999. Back Row L to R:- APFs David Healy, Mark O'Halloran, Alan Murphy, Olivia O'Gorman, Ann Golden, Jim O'Connor, Sean O'Farrell. Middle Row L to R:- APFs Shane Nugent, Padraigh. McCarthy, Neville Doyle, Brian Murphy, Denis Collins, Anthony Horan, Alan O'Leary. AFOs Arthur O'Leary, Pat Gallagher & Ger Harvey; Joe O'Connor Apt. Gen. Manager, Michael Healy CASO, Tony Murphy (AFO), Bertie Curtin (AFO).

*Photo – Aer Rianta Cork*

At retirement party for APFS Officer Dermot Collins in 1982.
At Back:- Ger Harvey, Mick Healy, Peter O'Neill. Front L to R:- Sean McSweeney, Con Buckley, Dermot Collins, Donie Harris, Jim Mulcare, John O'Mahony,Tommy Whelan, Pat Gallagher, Paddy Regan.

*Photo – Aer Rianta Cork*

therefore was necessary to the Airport Police Fire Service. By the end of 1999, twenty-four more recruits had gone through a rigorous induction training course, fourteen passing out in July and the remainder in December. These groups included, for the first time in the history of the force, four female officers. Again, due to early retirement and expansion, a further ten recruits were taken on in late 2000 and passed out in February 2001. This group also included two female officers bringing the total female officers in the force now to six. The period 1997-2001 was a hectic time for the Airport Police/Fire Service due to recruitment and training of forty-four young enthusiasts, bringing the total force to seventy eight.

Other exciting and positive things were also happening within the department during this time. In preparation for the large and still increasing numbers of passengers passing through the airport, it was felt that the supervisory grades within the force should be increased. In 2000, four officers were promoted to the rank of Station Officer in the Fire Service and ten officers promoted to the rank of Sergeant on the Police side. Also, one officer (Ray Shanahan) moved permanently to the C.A.S.O's office on a 9 to 5 Monday to Friday administration role. A break down of the force now stands:

Total staff strength 78
Chief Airport Security Officer.
Administration Officer.
6 Aerodrome Fire Officers.
4 Station Officers;
10 Police Sergeants.
56 Police/Fire personnel.

Passing out photograph of new recruits to the Airport Police/Fire Service December 1999. Back Row L to R:- APFs Rachel Lynch, Karen Roche, Lee Miles, Ray Dennehy, Andreas Fitzimmons. Middle Row L to R:- AFO Tony Murphy; APFs Don Cullinane, Gerard O'Sullivan, Ciaran Walsh, Ted Brady, Adrian Kevane; AFO Arthur O'Leary. Front Row L to R:- AFOs Ger Harvey, Mick Staunton; Joe O'Connor Airport General Manager; AFOs Pat Gallagher, Bertie Curtin.

*Photo – Aer Rianta Cork*

# Airport Police.

The security aspect of the service was more or less straightforward in the 1960s. Matters began to change with the eruption of the Northern Ireland troubles and of course international hijackings. Passenger screening was found to be necessary at all airports. Initially there was little or no concept of long-term security. However, this became necessary and airport security is now a top priority. Passengers eventually accepted it and in fact now demand it. All passengers boarding aircraft are now obliged to pass through a security clearance process on their way to the flight departure hall. This check includes inspection for valid boarding passes, hand-baggage x-ray, metal detection and physical checks where necessary and at random. This is the recognised method to ensure a safe flight passage for each passenger. Application of these procedures can vary for specific reasons.

The Airport Police service operates on a 24 hour, three-shift basis. All modern electronic aids are used in helping to maintain a high standard of policing including CCTV cameras. Mobile patrols monitor both the airport landside and airside constantly.

In general, three main elements exist to the airport policing operation, Passenger Screening, Traffic Flow and General Conduct. It is important that vehicular traffic is regulated in an orderly fashion to ensure the smooth operation for all. Vehicles utilising the airport come into different categories, e.g. long or short-term parking, car-hire, pick-up and drop-off, public service vehicles, deliveries, day trippers/sightseers and staff.

At an airport, there exists an operational difference between the landside, which the general public use and the airside or airfield area, which is restricted to a special catego-

Jerry O'Brien of the Airport Police/Fire Service seen singing a track from his tape, Autumn Light Musical Reflections at its launch at Cork Airport in 1990.
*Photo – Aer Rianta Cork*

ry of staff and passengers. Controlling these areas is an Airport Police function, which contributes to maintaining an efficient, functional and orderly airport.

As a general principle, the officers of the airport police section view the public with the following in mind - to give a professional courteous service and to respond positively to their needs. The public are the airport's main customers and pay good money for air transport facilities. It is appreciated that for some people, an airport can be a stressful place, e.g. funerals, celebrations, departing relatives, delayed appointments etc. and police officers are trained to deal with all such situations.

## Fire Service.

Apart from the security aspect, it has been seen how important the role of the Fire/Rescue Service has been through the years. Since the early days at the airport, many changes have come about. Standards under I.C.A.O. have been tightened. These created new requirements, not alone for personnel but for the fire vehicles being purchased to give greater fire fighting capacity. Accordingly, there were new designs of vehicles developed over the past decades. They have doubled in capacity and in the 1980s, the Irish-produced Timoney fire tenders came on the market. Aer Rianta supported this native initiative and in recent years invested over £5 million in them. These will be in use for the foreseeable future, creating greater standardisation at Irish airports. The major change in fire engine design has been that from the cab mounted engine to the rear motor engine vehicle now in operation. This was necessary to give greater engine power for greater operational capacity.

The original fire station at Cork Airport was used from October 1961 to 1972. Then, with the arrival of the first of the larger type of fire vehicle, the station was enlarged. These vehicles also required greater staff manning levels. For the first 12 months of the airport's existence, the fire station watch-room was in the Control Tower complex. It was subsequently moved to the roof of the fire station and in 1972 relocated to a more prominent position. A new fire station is planned for Cork Airport and should come on stream by the end of 2001

Training of personnel is an ongoing process in the Airport Fire Service and they regularly attend fire-fighting exercises in the purpose built fire ground at the airport. Here, aircraft simulators allow personnel to practice and perfect the techniques required to maintain this modern fully equipped service. In order to maintain and improve standards, all officers attend various instructor courses at the Civil Aviation Authority certified training college in Teesside in the UK.

Various types of extinguishing media for aircraft fire fighting are stipulated by I.C.A.O. and complied with. Some appreciation of costs involved may be of interest. A large fire engine (minimum of 2 for Cork Airport) costs approximately £600,000 at current prices and the smaller one £300,000. In terms of performance, the large ones carry 2400 gallons of water and 300 gallons of foam compound. They reach 80 kph in 40 seconds and discharge themselves completely in 2_ minutes. The smaller vehicles carry 900 gallons water and 50 gallons of foam compound. They reach 80 kph in 25 seconds and also discharge themselves in 21/2 minutes.

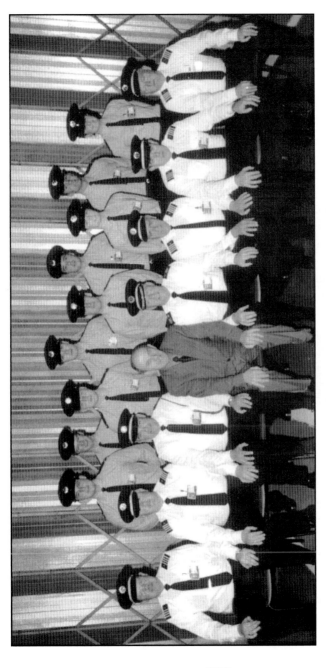

Passing out photograph of new recruits to the Airport Police/Fire Service 2001.
Back Row L to R:- APFs John McCarthy, Derek Coughlan, Steven O'Mahony, Charles Ponchon.
Middle Row L to R:- APFs Warren Delaforce, Gary Ryder, Richard Purcell, Bernadette O'Regan, Brian Curtin.
Front Row L to R:- AFOs Arthur O'Leary, Bertie Curtin, Ger Harvey; Joe O'Connor Airport General Manager;
Michael Healy C.A.S.O.; AFOs Pat Gallagher, Tony Murphy, Mick Staunton.
*Photo - Aer Rianta Cork.*

APFO Tom Kerrigan pictured with his wife Celia together with Michael Healy, CASO and Lilibeth Horne, Commercial Manager following his presentation of the Murphys Brewery Ambasador of Tourism award in association with Bord Failte and Shannon Development Sept, 1995. The prestigious award is designed to honour the individual who has demonstrated the Irish Welcome by making an outstanding contribution to the success of the Visitor Experience.
*Photo – John Sheehan Photography*

The Fire Service at the airport operates on a 24-hour basis, for the safety of passengers and property. By I.C.A.O. regulations, it provides fire vehicles of specific capacity, speed, output, efficiency levels, etc. Manning of these vehicles is a full time requirement. Operational practices, types of equipment and communications, disaster planning and search and rescue procedures are all regulated for.

On a daily basis, the fire crew carry out certain duties, when required, on the airfield. They are generally referred to as Field Duties and greatly influence safe operations on the airfield.

The Field Duties that the fire crews provide are as follows: -

1. Bird Hazard Issue. Keeping the airfield safe for aircraft operations by managing the bird hazard risk. Bird dispersal patrols are carried out regularly and when required.

2. Braking Tests. This is a process whereby the braking efficiency of a runway surface is measured. Certain weather conditions demand this type of information, e.g. snow or icy weather.

3. R.V.R. (Runway Visual Range). This is an operation, which requires a specific surface distance measurement during poor visibility conditions, (Cat. I and Cat. II). Pilots use this information for landing and take-off considerations. This operation is automated with three measuring devices at the touchdown point, mid point and end point on the main runway. Manual readings are taken if required.

4. Snowtams. This operation requires an exact statement on the prevailing runway conditions during snow conditions.

Group taken at retirement of APFO Jerry O'Brien 1st Nov. 1994.
Back Row L to R:-Mick McAuliffe, Tom Russell, Paddy Dempsey, Sean McSweeney John Milner, Denis Maher, Tom Kerrigan, Billy O'Keeffe, Barry Roche (Apt. Manager). Front Row L to R:-Mick Healy, Jerry O'Brien, Denis McSweeney, Mick Staunton Pat Gallagher, Donie Harris, Brendan Clancy, Kevin O'Farrell.

*Photo – Courtesy Brendan Clancy*

The result determines the usability of a runway during such periods.

5. Field Patrol. This practice requires airfield patrols to ensure an obstruction free runway and is also carried out for security needs.

6. Cat. II Checks. These airfield checks are carried out in poor weather conditions - horizontal visibility less than 1000 metres, forecast to fall below 800 metres and/or the cloud ceiling less than 300 ft. and forecast to fall below 200 ft. The airfield must be checked and cleared of non-essential personnel and equipment, making sure that all perimeter gates are locked and confirming that the LSA (Localiser Sensitive Area) on the landing runway is not compromised.

7. Water Checks. In wet weather conditions, inspections of the runways are carried out to determine what surface water exists and if there is any significant water lodgement. This information is then passed on to aircraft crews.

8. Escort Duties. All movements on the airfield of non-airport personnel such as contractors, delivery agents etc. must be escorted in the interest of security and safety.

As Cork Airport is part of the social/economic structure of this region, the Airport Police/Fire Service is proud to contribute to this concept for the general community.

Aer Rianta will process approximately 1.8 million passengers through Cork Airport by the end of 2001 and the Airport Police/Fire Service will have contributed in no small way to their safe passage and well being.

- - -

Today's modern Airport Police/Fire Service bears little comparison to that which existed on opening day. It is interesting, therefore, to look back and see how the service evolved. In The Story of Cork Airport (1988), a former Chief

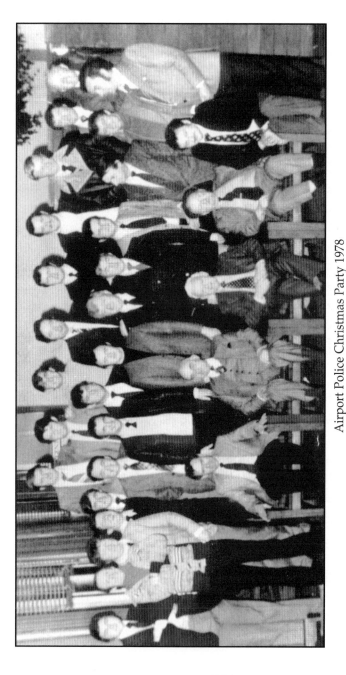

Airport Police Christmas Party 1978

Back Row L to R:- W. Murphy, T. O Beara, J. Mahony, T. Breathnach, J. Fitzgerald, B. Curtin, O. Jordan, L. O'Shea, T. O'Sullivan, J. Daly. Middle Row L to R:- G. Leonard, N. Bermingham, N. Kelly, T. Roche, D. Hayes, C. Buckley, P. O'Neill, J. Hyland, P. Walsh, M. O'Reilly, D. Harris, L. O'Shea, S. McSweeney,J. Lyons, P. O'Regan, Seated L to R:- P. Gallagher, S. Ryan, D. O'Keeffe, G. Holohan, A. Kenneally.

*Photo – Aer Rianta Cork*

Airport Security Officer Mick McAuliffe, who was a 'rookie' to the service in 1961 had this to say:

"For those involved in the early days of any major project, a special feeling exists. It is the feeling of hope, of new horizons, of being there at the start. A group of eager young men gathered together during the last days of September and the early days of October 1961. They were all new to each other; half were from outside the Cork area and the others a mixture of Cork City and County. All had different expectations but had a common binding spirit. These eleven, later extended to twenty-two within two years were to be Airport Wardens. The title grated. The work content was unknown. The reality of driving fire engines and regulating traffic soon became apparent. Driving fire engines was going to be some trick! Only one had previous heavy vehicle driving experience. None of the group had ever set foot in a fire engine and with only weeks to go to the official opening, the fire vehicles had not yet been delivered to the airport.

A Limerick man was given the task of training this group of young lions, aged between 19 and 24, into an airport fire service in a matter of weeks. His task was near impossible. To his credit, he nearly achieved that goal. He trained his men on an old fire vehicle which dated from the 1940s and his theory classes were given in an old farmhouse with its kitchen door as a blackboard.

The Limerick man, Gerard Tracey, deemed it part of his necessary training schedule to take this young undisciplined group on marching exercises. That was some sight to behold – young people attempting to co-ordinate their hands and feet to give the impression of a disciplined force. Our 'barrack square' consisted of unfinished runways, earth mounds, builders' rubble, concrete mixers etc. We had a permanent audience – the ESB group in their red Volkswagen pick-up were our chief supporters. We often wished that John, Billy and the rest of them would drive into a big hole and never surface again. Thankfully our wishes were not granted and with time firm friendships evolved.

Yes, we did learn to drive the new engines with their crash gear-boxes and heavy steering. We managed to speak a new language on R/T, differentiate between landside and airside, between the 17 end, ramp and taxiways, between a DC3, a Friendship and a Viscount. On the public side, we got the 'Deep End' treatment – regulating people through unfin-ished buildings, roads and car parks. That was a real maturing experience.

A week before the opening, it was realised that the Limerick Clothing Company would not have the uniforms ready for the big day. An emergency phone call to Shannon Airport produced a box of old uniforms from stores and following a quick dry cleaning job, were ready for use. Those who hadn't a uniform were given arm crests to wear over their civilian attire. Those uniforms were something spe-cial – not one fitted correctly and some had actual holes in them. Yet they were worn. It took many months before the official uniforms arrived.

Three Aer Rianta APFs from the class of '97 seen in front of the Aer Lingus "Tolar" which was promoting the new direct service to Amsterdam and Paris Charles de Gaulle Airport 5th June 1998. From left , Anthony Healy, Eoin Calnan and Sean McCarthy.

*Photo – Gabriel Desmond*

My lasting memory of opening day is of Gerry Holohan, then Assistant to the Airport Manager, 'restricting' the attendance to official invitees at the glass doors of the terminal building and the stampede across the now south ramp, which acted as a car park then, by the public when a DC3 was doing its run up prior to departure. The fire engines were brought into play to dampen the spirits of the public and eventually the aircraft got away safely and no one was injured.

Our strength in terms of numbers has grown. Over the years we have shared many happy memories. It is with satisfaction that I look back on the developing years and with confidence that I look forward to new horizons in the years ahead. To those who made my airport memories possible I say thank you, especially to those early dreamers who conceived the notion of Cork Airport. "

## CAR PARKING

Car parking at the airport has gone through a number of changes over the last 40 years. Those changes were influenced by growth, technology, customer demands, management style and changes in life style. In the early years it was seen as a facility for the customer and not much thought went into its importance as a means of generating revenue for the airport. Also, there were fewer cars in the country then.

In the early days the airport had a single 300 - space car park with car park charges on a time card basis operated from a caravan. That system changed in the early 1970s to a short-term car park of 100 spaces with a fixed rate of 50p per day and a long- term car park of 300 spaces with an unlimited stay for £4. This pay on exit system accepted 50p coins only.

The system was in operation until 1993 with very little change except that a number of extra spaces were provided in both car parks. 1993 saw the first major investment in car parking. Short-term parking was increased to 300 spaces and long-term parking to 800 spaces. Canopies were erected at the entrance and exit points. Payment machines, which calculated length of stay, were installed in the terminal. Car parking had become an important source of airport revenue. The short term daily rate rose to £5 and the long term rate rose to £12. However, business grew and demand for spaces in both the short-term and long-term car parks increased. This forced an increase in short-term spaces to 400 and long-term to 900 in 1997 and the opening of a grass area to facilitate demands during the busy summer period. This grass area could hold up to 1000 cars.

To date there are 400 short term and 900 long term spaces in car park No.1, both of which are full from May to October. There are also a further 1500 spaces in long-term car park No.2 and the same situation exists there during the busy period.

In 1994 a Car Park Services Office was opened in the terminal to give personal service to customers and by then the automatic payment machines were relocated there. Customers, should they so wish, can pay at the counter by cash, cheque or credit card. Value Cards are available and damaged tickets, and lost tickets are re-issued. The office also assists customers with difficulties including a complimentary jump-starting service. Personal attention is given to all customer queries and complaints.

Airport management have been looking at the overall car-parking situation and have seen the need for huge investment. A £12 million investment has been approved by Aer Rianta Board for a 600 space multi-storey car park, 300 extra short-term spaces, 400 extra spaces in long-term car park No.1 and up to 3000 spaces in long-term car park No. 2. These projects are currently in the design stage and are due to start in Sept. 2001. They will take approximately 9 months to complete and will cater for upwards of 3 million passengers per year. The cost to build will be between £8000 and £10,000 per space. The final phase of this project will be the creation of a shopping mall in the multi-storey car park where passengers and visitors can shop, have a meal and even have their hair styled. These facilities will make Cork airport a truly international airport capable of competing with the best.

- - -

As well as Aer Rianta, many other commercial and state agencies operate there. Each plays a vital part in the overall functioning of the airport.

## Irish Aviation Authority.

Based in the Control Tower complex at Cork Airport are the Irish Aviation Authority (IAA) Services and the Irish Meteorological Service. The IAA Services are Air Traffic and Engineering. They, together with the Aviation Marine Communications Service, which were formerly under the Air Navigation Services Office, came under the Irish Aviation Authority on 1st January 1994. The Management of the dif-

Albert Reynolds T.D., Minister for Transport pictured in the Control Tower Cork Airport during a visit on 5th June 1980 with L. to R. Gerry Holohan, Airport Manager, Paddy Bracken OIC Air Traffic Control, Padraig Flynn T.D., Minister of State, Dept. of Transport and Ray O'Keeffe, Controller.

*Photo - Courtesy Irish Examiner*

ferent groups within the new Authority remained relatively unchanged with controllers and engineers reporting via their own hierarchical arrangements to headquarters.

With the change of status, the opportunity was taken to set up a Commercial & Training Directorate to tender for external controller training and this has been very successful.

In 1997 KPMG, a consultancy company, was invited into the Authority to suggest ways of focussing the organisation in a more businesslike way. This focus was mainly in the Air Navigation area and it resulted in a restructuring of the organisation at all airports. There is now one Director of Air Navigation Services (ANS), Cyril McNamee, responsible for air traffic control, engineering and communications, There are General Managers at Dublin (Matt Bergin), Shannon (Mick Weldon) and Ballygireen (Pat Ryan) responsible for all activities. In Cork there is an ANS Manager (Sean McAdam O'Connell) who is responsible for all operational activities in the air traffic and engineering areas.

## Air Traffic Services.

Air traffic control is provided by Air Traffic Services staff. In additional to providing an air traffic control service at Cork, they also provide an Aeronautical Information Service (AIS) which provides flight planning and pre-flight briefing to air crew using Cork Airport. The functions of Air Traffic Control at Cork are basically twofold i.e. Approach Control Services and Aerodrome Control Services. Cork is provided with a Primary Surveillance Radar System, specially designed for Approach Control and airport surveillance applications. The system has a very high resolution, provides extensive coverage (60 nautical miles range over 360 degrees azimuth) whilst allowing for surveillance radar approaches to within

In 1994, the British Civil Aviation Authority won the contract for calibration of the navigation aids at Irish Airports, previously carried out by the US Federal Aviation Agency, FAA. These Hawker Sidley 748s later bore the name Flight Precision Ltd.

*Photo – Gabriel Desmond*

223

one nautical mile of touchdown of all airport runways and incorporates effective anti-clutter protection.

The Primary Radar's raw and synthetic data are displayed on autonomous 21" Plan View Displays (PVDs). In addition, synthetic data from the Monopulse Secondary Surveillance Radars sited at Mount Gabriel near Schull, Co. Cork is fed to these displays and controllers have the capability of inputting data on the PVD Keyboards to enable code-call sign correlation of the Mount Gabriel radar data. Cork Airport Control Centre Flight Data Positions are equipped with keyboards, electronic data displays and strip printers interfaced with the Shannon Airport Flight Data Processing System (FDPS) for the exchange of flight plan information and for access to the Aeronautical Fixed Telecommunications Networks (AFTN).

A dual Assmann real-time radar recording facility is installed as part of the radar system and also a Timeon time injection system.

These radar systems and automated facilities substantially enhance both the quality and quantity of information available for Air Traffic Control purposes at Cork.

An Instrument Landing System (ILS) is provided on both Runway 17 and Runway 35. ILS 17 is a Category II facility, which means a decision height for the pilot of 100 feet and ILS 35 is a Category I facility with a decision height of 200 feet. The provision of Category II ILS on Runway 17 has reduced aircraft diversions significantly.

Cork Approach provides ATC services for Cork Control Zone, which is, in turn, a sub-adjacent unit of the much larger Shannon Control Area. It has responsibility for an area embraced by a radius of 20 nautical miles from Cork Airport and up to a height of 6000 feet. This area constitutes the

Cork Control Zone. Cork Approach Control controls and separates all traffic within its area of responsibility. Included in this responsibility is the provision of an Aeronautical Information Service (AIS) and alerting a Search and Rescue Service for its own area of responsibility and/or any larger area under the direction of Shannon Area Control.

Aerodrome Control Service is provided by Tower Controllers and their responsibilities include the provision of separation between all movements on the aerodrome and in the Aerodrome Traffic circuit.

## Engineering Service.

The Engineering Service evolved from the Aviation Technical Operations Service, which in turn evolved from a restructuring of the Radio Service in 1975 and is part of the Irish Aviation Authority since 1994. It is an engineering and technical service whose functions are to ensure the operational reliability and accuracy of the ground based electronic equipment and telecommunication systems necessary for the regularity, efficiency and safety of air navigation. The electronic equipment, which the Technical Officer staff is responsible for includes all Radar facilities, Navigational Aids such as Instrument Landing Systems, Distance Measuring Equipment (DME) and Very High Frequency Omni directional Radio Range (VOR). The VHF Communications and Control Systems include the Main and Reserve Communications Equipment, and its Control and other ancillary facilities associated with it. These are built around computerised Central Control racks incorporating a comprehensive Information Display System (IDS), intercom and telephone systems together with a dual tape recorder system, a technical control desk including remote monitoring facili-

Albert Reynolds T.D. Minister for Transport, in the Radio Room Cork Airport 5th June 1980 with left, Derry Gearty OIC Radio Service and right Barra O Tuama, Aer Rianta Board member. In the background is Jack Riordan, Airport Engineer.

*Photo – Courtesy Derry Gearty*

ties and a diagnostic and system reconfiguration station. The technical staff is also responsible for the radio-synchronised clock system which drives console and wall clocks and for the Automatic Terminal Information System (ATIS) which is a stored speech VHF broadcast system and provides Air Traffic Control with a reliable means of continuously broadcasting details of Cork Airport landing conditions and other relevant information to aircraft.

The Technical Room is on the ground floor, in which is located the Communication Transmitters, Automatic Voice Recorders, Control Circuitry etc. Throughout the airfield, the Navigational Aids, Radar and VHF Receivers are housed in buildings identified by their international paint colouring of orange and white stripes. The main duties of the technical staff are:

(a) Ensuring and certifying that all equipment, which they are responsible for, is operating to the specifications, standards and tolerances laid down by International Civil Aviation (ICAO) standards and by the manufacturers, the diagnosis of faults and the restoration of equipment to operational service in the event of failure.

(b) Participating in and analysing and assessing the flight checking of equipment and reporting on its performance.

(c) Participating from time to time in the evaluation, commissioning and installation of new electronic equipment with representatives of manufacturers and other installation personnel.

In order to safeguard against failures of power supply to essential critical loads in the Air Traffic Control Environment, Uninterruptible Supply Systems (UPS) are installed. A

Air Traffic Controllers Brendan O'Sullivan and Gerard Cahill
in Approach Control at Cork Airport.
*Photo – Courtesy Cait Ward*

Des. Walsh and Matt McCormack of the Aviation Engineering
Service seen here among the computers.
*Photo –Courtesy Cait Ward*

228

Group of Communications Assistants ("Radio Girls") who came together to mark the closing of the Service at Cork Airport in May 1990. Back Row L to R:- Nuala Breen, Peggy Collins, Helen Long, Yvonne Whitley, Teresa O'Leary, Julienne O'Connor, Eileen Quinn. Centre Row L to R:- Kay O'Connell, Jenny Broderick, Josie O'Connor, Ann Finn, Sheila McCarthy, Lena O'Mahony, Mary Heaslip. Front Row L to R:- Cait Ward, Ann Walsh, Eileen Walsh, Patricia Laffin.

*Photo –Courtesy Cait Ward*

120KVA system supplies the Control Tower Equipment and a 60 KVA system supplies the Primary Radar site.

## Met Eireann (The Irish Meteorological Service)

The Meteorological Service's involvement at Cork Airport began at the Ballygarvan site when preliminary monitoring of the weather was carried out there from September 1946 to June 1947.

When the airport opened in 1961, the Met. Office provided routine weather observations as required by International Civil Aviation Organisation  Regulations for Aircraft. Towards the end of that year, observations were made on a 24 hour basis and the station became part of a nation-wide network of climatological stations supplying weather data for non-aviation as well as aviation statistics.  There was no forecasting service available from the airport itself; instead Mufax Receivers were installed to receive the weather charts from the Central Forecasting Office and by Shannon. However, as air traffic built up much quicker than expected, a forecast section was opened at Cork Airport in 1966 under Donal Linehan, who later became Director of the Irish Met. Service.

In December 1988, Cork and Dublin ceased to be forecast offices and Shannon Airport became the Central Aviation Office, assuming forecasting responsibility for all Irish airports.

The public dimension of the work of the Met. Office at Cork Airport took on a special significance from the 1970s onwards as public awareness of the value of weather forecasts grew.  This led to the installation of an automatic

This photo was taken at Cork Airport in the Spring of 1989 following the closure of the meteorological forecast office in December 1988. The occasion was the retirement of five members of the Service. Back Row L to R:- Denis Cahill, John Scanlon (Retired.), Brian Doyle, Eddie Kelly, Sean McAuliffe, John Collins, Tom Maunsell, Dave Murphy, Oliver Veale (Retired.) Denis Cahalane. Front Row L to R:- Dominic Finn (Retired.), Cormac O'Connor O.I.C.(Retired.), Michael Murtagh, Frank Fitzgerald (Retired.), Peter Hawkes.

*Photo – Courtesy Cait Ward*

231

answering telephone service in 1982 on which was recorded a five day weather forecast for the area. It handled a total of 47,500 calls in the first year. By the end of 1991 the calls numbered 733,000. During 1992 this service was discontinued and replaced by a premium rate service and though definite figures for this service are not available, it continues to be very popular with the general public. Calls reach their peak between May and August inclusive each year when haymaking and harvesting are involved.

On 1st January 1997, after a trial period of five months, a meteorological self-briefing service was made available near the Aer Rianta Duty Office, which is used by airline and private pilots.

In March 2000, the Dines anemometer masts, which for so long had been a feature of the skyline on the right-hand side as you drove into the airport, were finally dismantled. They had been in official service from 1961 until the mid 1990s when they were replaced by more modern electronic anemometers. However, it is hoped that parts that were salvaged during the dismantling can be used to build a working model in the Foynes Aviation Museum.

The Officer-in-Charge of the Met Office in Cork is Brian Doyle.

- - -

As referred to earlier in this book, Michael (Mickey) Murtagh, the first OIC of the Met. Service at Cork Airport made the initial weather observations in September 1946 to June 1947 at Lehenaghmore (part of the airport site now). Observations were also made at Ahanesk, Midleton. Both locations were contenders for the airport site. The Ballygarvan site, as it was called, eventually became the choice.

A former Cork Airport Manager, Gerry Holohan, contributed the following pen-portrait for this book of Michael, which he called 'Michael Murtagh – An All-Weatherman'.

"When a well-groomed Meteorological Officer materialises on your T.V. screen and then shepherds weather troughs and ridges from mid-Atlantic as far as the Bosphorus, that may well be the only contact or view of the people in the Met. Service you may ever get. Their performance is professional and focussed; personnel in that service are multi-talented and of high technical ability. Having worked and lived with Met. personnel at both Shannon and Cork Airports, I was fortunate to get close to the persona and character of a small number of these specialist Civil Servants.

Mickey Murtagh first saw the light of day on 24th Sept. 1920 and was one of seven children. Following his early education at Crosshaven Convent Primary School and Myrtleville National School, he attended secondary school at CBS North Monastery where as a Leaving Cert. Student he shared a desk with a future Taoiseach, the late Jack Lynch. He sat the Civil Service Examination for posts in the Meteorological Service in 1938 and was called for training as a Met. Assistant in March 1939.

Mick had training periods in Dublin and Valentia Met. Station before appointment to Foynes (Shannon), just prior to the start of the 1939-'45 war. As operations required, Mick and colleagues would shuttle to Rineanna across the river from Foynes and today's Shannon Airport – to service land planes as opposed to sea-planes which then spanned the

Atlantic. Foynes Sea-Plane Base was run on a semi-military security basis, and military were at the nearby Mt. Trenchard Garrison. Mick married in 1943 and settled in Limerick.

In September 1946 he and family were transferred to Cork where he served at the Lehenaghmore observation site and later at Ahanesk. During the infamous three-month snow and freeze-up (January-April 1947), Mick travelled to and from work on a trusted Raleigh bike. He was transferred from Ahanesk to Shannon Airport in 1956. While in Ahanesk he commuted daily by bike from Cork initially and later from Cloyne. His latter years in Cloyne were graced with - his quote -"a dreadful old banger of a car".

The cheerful Murtagh character arrived at the by then Shannon Airport (Rineanna) in 1956, when I first met him, and from then until September 1961 he lived in the staff hostels at Shannon, commuting to his family in Cork for his "off or "rest" days. Some three or four weeks prior to Cork Airport opening on 16th October 1961, Mick was sent south and home to oversee the commissioning of the Met. Station at Cork Airport. My main memory of Murtagh at this time was of the frustrations he and Foreman Electrician, John Drennan, suffered in the installation of the DINES Anemometer Masts. Drennan, to this day, says he does not need a Bible to swear on the Anemometer problems. The installation was done on time and that equipment functioned well until replaced by more modern apparatus in the mid-1990s. Well done lads!

Murtagh for me was the living, walking and colourful talking bridge between the romance of the Atlantic Flying Boats and the big precision flying machines, such as, the Boeing 747 and other Jumbo Jets. Foynes in the 1940s saw the two North Atlantic colossi - Pan-Am's Charlie Blair and Imperial Airway's Kelly-Rogers. Mick Murtagh was contemporary with the Irish Aviation legends Con McGovern, Ned Stapleton, Jim Devoy, Col. Paddy Maher - Airport Manager, Denis Herrity - Marine Rescue and Harry Boyle, automotive expert.

On return to Cork in 1961, Mick and his family continued to live at Hoddersfield, a mile up-river from Crosshaven. He retired from the Met. Service on the 31st July 1981. Now a widower, he is active, mobile and as cheerful and positive as ever he was. In his home at Hoddersfield he continues to live beside and to hear, the lapping waters of the estuarine Owenabue. He can hear the plaintive curlews' cry; at night in the stillness he may hear a dog-fox bark; and by day he can hear the joyous peals and cheers of his grandchildren nearby.

Murtagh, a weatherman by profession, but truly a man of many great seasons! God Bless you Micheál - it's been good to know you!"

# 6

# CHAPTER SIX

## Airlines Serving Cork Airport

In 2001, Cork Airport is expected to handle about 1.8 million passengers. Ireland's rapid economic growth and the deregulation of the airline industry has meant that people now readily travel for reasons of business, holiday or visiting friends and relations.

Aer Lingus, still state-owned, is the only airline that has continuously served Cork Airport over its forty years and in 2001 had routes to London Heathrow, Dublin, Birmingham, Amsterdam and Paris. Frankfurt is served on one-stop flights through Dublin. Since it disposed of its last Fokker 50s early in 2001, Aer Lingus is once more an all-jet airline, still flying Boeing 737 series 400 and 500 but gradually phasing in the slightly bigger Airbus 321 and 320 series, with the Airbus 319 on order. Their Aer Lingus Commuter subsidiary uses British Aerospace Bae 146s jets on the Birmingham route. In addition to scheduled flights, Aer Lingus Airbuses fly overnight to Faro, Ibiza and Las Palmas on weekend charters in summer. Other Irish airlines are Ryanair who have 4 daily London Stansted flights and Aer Arann who have three ATR42 flights per day to Dublin, in association with Aer Lingus.

British Airways colours are a common sight at Cork Airport, all carried by subsidiaries or franchise partner airlines. CityFlyer have 3 daily London Gatwick flights; Brymon fly to Plymouth, Bristol and Newcastle and British Regional serve Manchester, Glasgow and Jersey.

British European, up to recently known as Jersey European, links Cork to Birmingham twice a day, using Dash 8 or BAe 146 aircraft. Air Wales have 2 daily Cardiff flights, with the Dornier 228 and Keenair fly from Liverpool at week-ends using a Banderiante.

Summer sees a huge increase in holiday charter flights and some seasonal scheduled routes, mostly to destinations in the Mediterranean or the Canary Islands. Futura, the Spanish airline, are partly owned by Aer Lingus and in 2001 served Tenerife, Malaga, Las Palmas, Lanzarote, Mahon and Palma, plus Heraklion in Crete, using Boeing 737 400s and 800s. Other airlines bringing sun worshippers to Spain were Air Europa, Iberworld and Spanair, to Alicante, Reus and Malaga plus some destinations already mentioned. Faro Airport in southern Portugal is the gateway to the Algarve coast and Air Luxor, Euro Atlantic and Air 2000 all fly there from Cork. Air 2000 also have charters to Almeria in Spain.

Other Mediterranean summer routes are Air Malta to Malta, using their new Airbus 319, Air Littoral to Monastir in Tunisia, Pegasus to Bodrum in Turkey and Euro Cypriot to Larnaca. Westair have a summer route to Quimper in Brittany and Crossair bring Swiss visitors from Zurich.

Pilgrim flights are less frequent but are a traditional feature of the annual travel pattern. Destinations include Lourdes in southern France, Medjugore in Bosnia Herzegovina, often reached through Split in Croatia, and for the Holy Land to Tel Aviv on Boeing 757s of El Al.

Since the main runway was extended, Lourdes flights have brought the biggest planes to land at Cork. There have

Five Aer Lingus baggage handlers in jovial mood.13th April 1995.
From the left they are Jim Finn, Martin Walsh,
John Cronin, Pat Whyte, John Burns.
*Photo – Gabriel Desmond*

been visits by Boeing 747 Jumbos of Aer Lingus and Air Atlanta of Iceland who have also used Tristar wide bodies. Tristars of Caledonian, Air Ops, Peach and Classic have all appeared on Lourdes charters. Other wide bodies came on charters from France and Spain – DC10s of Air Outre Mer and Airbus 300s of Air Liberte and Trans Aer. The longer runway also made it possible for former Eastern Block jets such as the Tupelov 154 and YAK42 to make occasional charter flights to Cork.

On the north side of the airport, three express freight companies – DHL, UPS and TNT, operate specialised freighter aircraft, which carry overnight freight to the UK and beyond. These are usually windowless Boeing 727F or BAe 146 aircraft with large side doors. The freight is loaded in igloo-shaped "cans". They fly out at about 8pm and return by 8am. Aer Lingus also process air freight at the freight base.

To complete the picture of regular air traffic at Cork in 2001, there are oil rig support flights from Aberdeen by Highland Express with a Dornier 228. CHC, formerly known as Bond Helicopters, use their red Dauphin helicopter on daily flights for Marathon Petroleum to the offshore platform of the Kinsale Gas Field. The private Hawker business jets of EMC ferry clients from all over Europe to visit their electronic components manufacturing plant at Ovens. These jets are based at the hangar vacated by Irish Helicopters. Incidentally, Irish Helicopters still visit with the Bolkow Bo 105, which is used for coastal lighthouse re-supply.

In 2001, there were 130,000 summer charter seats available, 30,000 more than in the year 2000. Unfortunately, due to a Foot and Mouth outbreak, five Boston charter flights to Cork Airport this summer were cancelled. However, this initial series of flights will be made next year and will open the door for further charters from Boston and New York in the years ahead.

## Aer Lingus.

Aer Lingus, the national airline, commenced services in May 1936 with a De Havilland Dragon called the Iolar. The first flight was on May 26th from Dublin to Bristol and carried only five passengers. In 1999, the airline carried over 5.8 million passengers and 45 tonnes of cargo to 35 different cities in 13 different countries.

Today, Aer Lingus operates a schedule suited to both the business and leisure traveller and offers a quality for money product. The airline currently operates one of the most modern fleets in Europe, this includes A320, A321, A330, B737 and BAe 146 Jet aircraft.

Aer Lingus, as already mentioned, is the only airline that has continuously served Cork Airport since it opened in October 1961. In 2000, it handled a throughput of 1.2 million passengers at Cork and that figure is expected to reach 1.5 million by the end of 2001. It now offers from Cork, scheduled services directly or through Dublin to 9 UK airports, 15 to Continental Europe and 6 US Gateways, which include New York (JFK and Newark), Boston, Chicago, Los Angeles and Baltimore. Direct services to Amsterdam, Paris-CDG, and Birmingham complement the increased capacity on the Cork-Heathrow route, which is now operated by A321 aircraft.

Aer Lingus now employs over 150 staff and management at Cork, which includes a sales team headed by District Sales Manager Mary Purcell and Cargo headed by Michael Bolger. The airline is working closely with Aer Rianta who are com-

Denise O'Sullivan, Aer Lingus Ground Hostess, Cork Airport seen here
having been crowned 1992 Rose of Tralee.
*Photo – Courtesy Irish Examiner*

Tom Ringrose and Donie Ford of Aer Lingus Cork Airport, both sadly now deceased, shown deep in conversation in 1992

*Photo – Aer Rianta Cork*

242

mitted to investing £61m in improvements at Cork Airport. Aer Lingus is complementing this by extending its dedicated Gold Circle lounge. This will offer increased and upgraded facilities, which will be manned by Aer Lingus personnel on a daily basis.

While the number one priority for all customers is punctuality, business customers at Cork as well as the Gold Circle facility, are now offered dedicated check-in facilities, the highest priority in boarding and disembarkation and priority baggage delivery at their destination.

Business passengers at Cork can now also avail of the "Ticket Book" which offers the Corporate customer ten fully flexible business tickets which can be used by anyone in a Company at a potential cost saving of 30%. They can also enjoy the benefits of the Aer Lingus frequent flyer programme TAB, designed to reward loyal customers by offering free flights, flight upgrades and an exclusive range of high quality gifts.

Aer Lingus handles the majority of Third Party Handling customers operating into Cork and continues to offer the highest level of passenger handling, loading and unloading of aircraft, including cargo and full maintenance cover.

In charge of the Aer Lingus operation at Cork Airport is Brian Cox.

## Ryanair.

Ryanair, which is now firmly established as Europe's largest low fares airline, began operations in 1985 using a 19 seat Bandeirante with the launch of a daily flight between Waterford and Gatwick. Then they used the bigger Hawker Sidley HS 748 on Waterford-Luton. They diverted to Cork

Ryanair staff in 1992
Back Row L to R:- Fiona Healy, Sally-Ann Irwin, Breda McCarthy (Noonans Cleaners),
Lydia Crotty. Front Row L to R:- Andrew Collins, Alan Long, Eamon Cassdy, Brian O'Donoghue, Ray O'Mahony,
David O'Donovan, John Paul Quinn, Dan Cassidy.
*Photo – Courtesy Alan Long*

when the weather at Waterford was poor. The Company carried 5,000 passengers on the Gatwick route in its first year. Later, the Bandeirante was used for the overnight express mail flights of An Post from Cork.

In 1988, Ryanair began flying from Cork to Luton using BAC 1-11 jets.   At that time, a route licence was still necessary from both governments. The Irish authorities quickly granted the licence but the UK were reluctant to grant Ryanair a Luton-Cork licence in addition to the Luton to Dublin route. So Ryanair initially flew from Cork to Luton with a technical landing at Dublin en route, adding to the time and expense but determined to make their point.

They placed an early order for two of the new Airbus 320 but never took delivery.  Airbus brought a test aircraft F-WWDC, with Ryanair titles on one side and Airbus titles on the other, on a promotional flight to Cork on 14th March 1988.  From 1989 to 1992, Ryanair flew 2 ATR 42s from the new regional airports at Waterford and Kerry. In 1990, their schedule included a Kerry-Cork-Luton route.

By 1994, Ryanair had selected Stansted as their London airport, using Boeing 737-200s.  Some of these were painted in sponsored colour schemes for Jaguar cars, The Sun Newspaper and a brilliant yellow for Hertz Car Hire. To date, they have carried over 1.5 million passengers on that route.

Under a new management team, a major overhaul of the Company was undertaken in 1990/'91 and a sleek and trimmer Ryanair was re-launched as the very first new breed of "low fares/ no frills" airline.   This new competitive downward pressure on the general level of air fares greatly helped to popularise air travel.  Other cost cutting measures includ-

Ryanair pilots and Corkmen, Willie Casey (left) and his cousin Mark Casey
with the new Ryan Boeing 737-800 at Cork Airport in August 1999.
*Photo – Gabriel Desmond*

ed the early introduction of website booking and the phasing out of the need to issue paper air tickets.

At busy holiday periods such as Christmas, Easter and August, Ryanair often hired in bigger aircraft such as Boeing 757s from Monarch or even bigger Airbus 300s from Translift or European Airlines of Belgium.

With their phenomenal growth since 1985, Ryanair now have 45 routes across Europe and employ 1400 people. Their fleet of 31 aircraft carry over 7 million passengers a year. In 2001, Ryanair had four daily flights from Cork to Stansted, which increasingly used the new 737-800.

## British Airways.

The airline was formed in 1972 with the amalgamation of British Overseas Airways Corporation (BOAC) and British European Airways (BEA). Although the airline did from time to time operate charter flights to Cork, it wasn't until April 1976 that British Airways took over scheduled services on the Cork-London Heathrow route, formerly operated by Cambrian Airways. They operated a very successful service using aircraft such as Viscounts, Tridents, BAC 1-11s, Boeing 737s and occasionally the larger Boeing 757. The company continued operations until 24th March 1991.

## CityFlyer

CityFlyer is a wholly owned subsidiary of British Airways Plc and has operated the Cork to London Gatwick services on behalf of British Airways since March 1995. That company began as Euroworld Airways in 1991 and the following January changed its name to CityFlyer Express. In July 1993, a major new marketing agreement with British Airways was announced. All CityFlyer scheduled services adopted British Airways Express branding from 1st August 1993 and operated under a franchise agreement with British Airways. A repainting programme to put the existing fleet into British Airways colours began.

CityFlyer began operating on the Cork-Gatwick route with ATR72 and ATR42 aircraft on 26th March 1995. In May 1997, they introduced Avro RJ100 jets on to this route. In November 1998, a conditional agreement for British Airways to purchase 100% of the shares in CityFlyer was announced and in November 1999, the sale agreement with British Airways was completed. CityFlyer continued to trade as a separate company but British Airways replaced the existing institutional and management shareholders.

Currently, CityFlyer operates a mixture of ATR72 and RJ100 aircraft from Cork.

## Brymon Airways.

Brymon Airways operated their first commercial flight in 1972 from Newquay in Cornwall to the Scilly Isles using a nine-seater Britten-Norman Islander. The airline moved its base from Newquay to Plymouth in 1973 and began scheduled flights from there to Cork Airport in 1975 using Islander aircraft. As traffic built up Twin Otter planes were used. In 1982, Brymon became UK launch customer for the De Havilland Canada Dash 7 aircraft and used them for many years on the Cork – Plymouth route during the busy periods.

Over the years, the company expanded and developed many major routes. In 1993 Brymon Airways became a wholly owned subsidiary of British Airways and it was

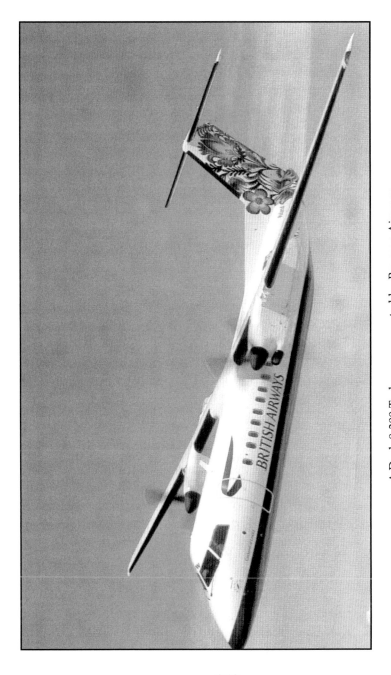

A Dash 8-300 Turboprop operated by Brymon Airways.
*Photo – Courtesy Brymon Airways*

announced that it would trade under the British Airways name. The company kept its fleet well updated purchasing five Dash 8-300 aircraft in 1996 to replace the Dash 7 and Dash 8-100 planes. Two more Dash 8-300s were purchased in 1997 and in 1998 an order worth £60m was placed with Bombardier in Canada for 8 Dash 8Q-300 aircraft.

In February 2000, Brymon took delivery of its first Embraer ERJ145 at Bristol and by the end of the year six of them were in service operating new and existing routes throughout the Brymon Airways network and operating services from Birmingham on behalf of British Airways Regional. The jets were purchased from Embraer in Brazil with options on a further 14 aircraft. The order and options on the 21 aircraft is valued at $420m.

Brymon Airways have given excellent service to Cork Airport for over 25 years and fly there from both Plymouth and Bristol. An expansion of their services to Cork in 2001 began on February 26th from four times per week to every day in the week. Also, a new daily service between Cork-Newcastle was launched on 25th March. One of the big changes on these new services was the first-ever two-class offering on their 50-seat Dash 8 turbo prop aircraft providing both Club Europe and Euro-Traveller facilities to their customers.

# British Regional Airlines.

In 1994, Manx Airlines, who with Loganair, were part of the British Midland Group, began twice daily scheduled flights from Manchester to Cork. Soon renamed British Regional, they used Jetstream 41 aircraft, as well as BAe 146s and ATPs. In 1997, British Regional became the first UK customer for

Servisair staff pictured 6th June 1997 on their first official day as second handler at Cork Airport. Back Row L to R:- Alan Long (Manager), Frank Walsh, Ray O'Mahony, Oonagh Hughes, Elmarie Coogan, Geraldine Byrne, Sharon O'Mahony, Karen O'Mahony, Keith Hutchinson, Neil Henderson. Front Row L to R:- Pat Cassidy, Kieran Russell, Eamon Cassidy, John Quinn.

*Photo –Courtesy  Servisair*

the Embraer EMB 145, the 50 seat jet made in Brazil. In 2001, they had three daily flights from Manchester and one from Glasgow, with an additional 2 weekend flights to Jersey in the summer. All services are operated in British Airways colours under a franchise agreement.

## Servisair.

Servisair, Europe's largest independent Ground Handling Agent, commenced operations at Cork in March 1993. Initially, it provided only Cargo handling for a number of airlines and freight agents.

In June 1997, it officially commenced passenger handling at Cork. The start-up customers for that operation were British Airways CityFlyer and Ryanair. Servisair now employs approximately 50 staff at the Cork station and provides full passenger and cargo handling. A number of the main services provided are passenger check-in and ticketing, meeting and greeting, aircraft boarding, handling of special assistance passengers, baggage/cargo offload and onload, aircraft cleaning and aircraft servicing. It also operates a bonded warehouse at the Cargo Terminal at Cork where handling services are provided.

Servisair's core cargo customers are DHL, TNT and UPS who have daily flights from Cork Airport. Its core passenger customers at Cork are Ryanair and the three British Airways franchise carriers CityFlyer, British Regional Airlines and Brymon Airways.

Servisair also provides handling for a number of charter airlines, mainly Westair, Aeris, Euro Atlantic, Air 2000, Air Luxor, Euro Cypria and Iberworld. It also handles a large number of private flights at Cork Airport. The Servisair manager in Cork is Alan Long.

## Customs.

Since the introduction of The Single Market in 1993, the thrust of Customs Control has changed considerably. Now, "Intra-Community" passengers (coming from another Member State of the EU) are not normally subject to any Customs restrictions and can exit through the Blue Channel. Duty Free sales to these travellers have been abolished.

Customs at Cork Airport consists of :

(a) Airport staff who deal with day-to-day issues including the clearance of non- EU passengers, Freight etc.

(b) Enforcement staff whose brief is Anti-Smuggling (Drugs, Cigarettes, Counterfeit Goods etc.) They operate on a system of targeting flights and/or individuals based on Risk Analysis, Profiling and general intelligence work.

## Catering

The absence of catering facilities in the early months following the opening of the airport posed problems, not alone for the travelling public but also for staff, many of whom were obliged to work shift duties. Aer Lingus staff probably fared better than most at that time, even if it was expensive for them, as soup and sandwiches were flown from Dublin.

Once the catering facilities and bar were ready in the Spring of 1962, the franchise was obtained by the Great Southern Hotels, then the catering side of CIE. Harringtons Catering Company obtained the concession in 1964 and held it until Bewleys took over in January 1992. In the summer of

2000, the franchise was split, Kylemore obtained the bar and airport catering franchise and Alpha the flight catering.

Kylemore had been established in 1987 and quickly gained a reputation for quality and service. A 100% Irish owned business "Kylemore Foods Group Ltd" is an associate company of D.C.C. plc. Kylemore is a successful, progressive group broadening its horizons in the catering business. They have 10 cafes throughout Ireland, serve over 5 million customers annually and employ over 500 people.

At Cork Airport, Kylemore are developing the first floor level to incorporate a food village and Bar/Lounge facility as well as a new enlarged Bar/Café in the Departures Lounge. On the ground floor, there will be a "Coffee Kiosk" that will serve convenience beverages and food. The developments will provide a total experience of luxury and indulgence using a mixture of traditional and modern designs and food concepts, a first class experience.

As part of their development programme, Kylemore plan to introduce new concepts and offerings of an international flavour as well as their traditional fare of quality and variety. The ambience and customer experience will be an expression of quality and convenience. Outward bound, on arrival or as a casual visitor, all will be met with a catering offer to exceed their expectations.

## Aviation Fuel

Up to May 1983, aviation fuel for Cork Airport was supplied by Irish Shell (formerly Shell and BP). The company discontinued its services and one of its employees, Gerry O'Donnell, took over the franchise on 1st May 1983 and formed Sky Fuel Ltd. The new company continued to supply Shell aviation fuel.

In 1997, Gerry O'Donnell retired after 42 years service with Shell Aviation and Sky Fuel Ltd. He was one of those who began work at Cork Airport in September 1961 and remained there until his retirement.

Shell Aviation returned to the airport in a new role and all operations are now carried out by an agent, Sky Fuel Aviation Ltd., which is run by Gerald O'Donnell Jnr. Shell upgraded the facilities and built a modern into-plane facility on the site. The company carries two grades of aviation fuel, Jet A-1 and Avgas 100LL. Storage has been increased at the site. Sky Fuel Aviation Ltd. covers all the operating hours of Cork Airport and gives fulltime employment to nine people.

In 1998, due to growth at the airport, Shell in conjunction with Sky Fuel Retail Ltd. built a modern Petrol Station there.

# Bank of Ireland

The Bank of Ireland opened a sub-office at Cork Airport in May 1971 following the granting of the franchise to them for the three State airports. Prior to that, the Ulster Bank was based there. For many years, the bank, which was located where the Aer Lingus ticket desk is now situated, opened for approximately three hours a day on week days only.

The bank moved to a new location beside the public shop in 1988 and a Pass ATM machine was installed in 1990. During this time, opening hours were considerably longer and Saturday and Sunday opening commenced. Today, Bureau facilities are available up to 14 hours per day, throughout the week including Sundays. A Foreign Currency machine is in operation on a 24 hour basis.

Among those in charge over the years were Tony Fitzgerald, Mick Walsh, Tony O'Malley, Joe Parker, Des Grealy, Rhona Brennan, Ann Carey and Joe Fogarty. The bank has always held only sub-office status, at first from the Patrick Street branch and later from Wilton. In 2001, it is being upgraded to full branch status. At present it has a staff of six, new Manager John O'Donnell, Des Grealy, Geraldine Hughes, Laura O'Leary, Maeve Joyce and Valerie Williams.

## Airport Shop

The airport "sky shop", as distinct from the travel value and tax free shops is operated on a concession basis. The present concessionaires are Conor and Mary Crowley. The shop provides an excellent service, stocking all the items one may require when travelling including papers, books and magazines.

## Car Hire

The car hire firms at Cork Ariport are Avis, National, Hertz, Budget and Europe Car. There are also two desks for pre-booked cars. Desk 'A' is for Dooley/Malone Car Hire and Desk 'B' for Sixth Car Hire.

## Helicopter Activity

Commercial helicopter activity commenced at Cork Airport in the early 1970s when Irish Helicopters Ltd., a subsidiary of British Air Services began its involvement with off shore explorations and leased large helicopters to support that work off the south coast. At that stage, Marathon and Esso

In 1996, Bond Helicopters, won the Marathon Petroleum contract for supplying the Kinsale Field gas platforms. using Aerospatiale SA365N Dauphin, EI-MIP.

*Photo – Gabriel Desmond*

Bell 212, EI-BFH, disembarking workers from the Kinsale Gas Field in July 1992. For over twenty years, Irish Helicopters ferried crews to and from the two production platforms, Alpha and Bravo, for Marathon Petroleum.

*Photo – Gabriel Desmond*

were the only companies involved in explorations in Irish waters. In 1974, Aer Lingus purchased a majority interest in the Company and Irish Helicopters Ltd. bought its first Bell 212 helicopter for exploration purposes. Their activities at Cork Airport were now considerable and business greatly increased when Marathon Petroleum began development of the Old Head of Kinsale Gas Field in 1977. In June of that year, Aer Lingus bought out the minority shareholder and became sole owner. Irish Helicopters Ltd. bought its second Bell 212 machine and Marathon erected a helicopter hangar to house them.

The construction of the gas-producing platforms was the first all year operation for the Company since its engagement in a lighthouse relief contract in 1969. During 1976-'78, there was tremendous activity due to the massive movement of material and personnel connected with the gas rig. In the late 1970s, drilling results, particularly those of Philips and BP, suggested that the Porcupine would be the area for further development. Prompted by this and the distance off shore, the Company acquired a Sikorsky S61 (26 passengers) in 1979 and another in 1981. A large hangar and office complex, the Company's main operational and engineering base, was opened on 15th June 1981. Irish Helicopters Ltd. built it at a cost of £400,000, Aer Rianta having leased the site to them.

In February 1996, Bond Helicopters (Ireland) Ltd, was awarded a long-term contract by Marathon Petroleum (Ireland) Ltd. to provide a helicopter service to Marathon's two Kinsale platforms Alpha and Bravo. This contract commenced on 1st April 1996 utilising a twin engine IFR Eurocopter Dauphin 365N helicopter. A workforce of ten is employed at Cork Airport where the company has administrative and hangar facilities. Daily flights take place ferrying offshore workers and materials to the Kinsale Gas Field. The helicopter, call sign EI-MIP, has a range of 400 nautical miles and can carry up to ten passengers.

Bond Helicopters (Ireland) Ltd. was established in May 1994 as a wholly owned subsidiary of Bond Helicopters Ltd. based at Aberdeen, Scotland. In 1997 they became part of the Helicopter Service group of Norway. In 1999, CHC Helicopter Corporation purchased the Helicopter Service/Bond group of companies. CHC Helicopter Corporation is the world's most geographically diverse helicopter service company in the world, operating a fleet of more than 300 aircraft in 21 countries.

In October 2000, Bond Helicopters (Ireland) Ltd. was renamed CHC Ireland.

## Flying Club

The Cork Aero Club or Flying Club was founded in 1934 and went out of existence in 1943. There was no flying club in Cork from then until the late 1950s when the Cork Flying Club was formed and they began flying at Farmers Cross airfield. The club later changed its name to the Munster Aero Club. The Club staged a famous race there for the Shell Trophy in 1960. Following the opening of Cork Airport, the Club took a 25 years lease on a site there in 1962. It had four permanent directors, Johnny Gray, Brian Reidy, Tony Doyle and Denis Joyce.

The latter was one of the early Club instructors who also held an Aircraft Engineer's licence. A few years after operations began at the airport, Denis Joyce established Joyce Aviation Ltd. to conduct aircraft maintenance/flying activities from the former club hangar and acquired the lease of the Club site. He in turn sub-let the Club House back to the Munster Aero Club, which was officially opened on 29th March 1964.

On 16th September 1965, Group Captain Douglas Bader, CBE, DSO, DFC, the famous World War 2 air ace was made an honorary life member of the Club on the occasion of his visit to Cork.

Throughout the '60s and early '70s, the Munster Aero Club conducted flying instruction and general aviation activities using at various stages, Auster, Bolkow Jimnor, Piper, Colt, Rallye, Piper Cherokee and Grumman Traveller aircraft. An oil crisis at the end of 1973 led to a serious escalation in flying costs, with consequent reduction in flying activity in 1974 and 1975. Following severe gale damage in 1975, the hangar had to be replaced.

The emergence of group purchased aircraft saw a renewed increase in activity from 1976 until 1986 and a number of new flying groups emerged including Cork Flying Group, Liberty Flying Group, Leeside Flying Group and the Hibernian Flying Club. During this period, the aircraft fleet consisted of a Cessna150 and a Piper Cherokee and for a short period a Cessna 210 and Piper Arrow.

Aer Rianta took over the entire complex including the hangar in 1986. The changing face of flight training/licencing requirements saw the need for a full-time commercially run flight training school. Realising this, South Aer was established in 1993 with the Club premises providing an operating base until South Aer's relocation to much larger accommodation at the south side of the hangar in 1998. The part-time flight instruction, conducted by Munster Aero Club, which for so many had provided the early steps to a

The late Hugh Coveney T.D. Minister of State and Jack Higgins, Cork City Manager at the opening of the new freight terminal at Cork Airport in Nov. 1995

*Photo – Aer Rianta Cork*

commercial flying career, is no longer feasible. All Club flying ceased in 2000 when the Liberty Flying Group sold its Rallye 150 aircraft, whilst the former club hangar is now home to CHC Helicopters.

## Freight.

Cargo plays a vital role in the future of Cork Airport. A new cargo village south of the airport on 40 acres will be developed over the next five years serving existing and new cargo customers. Over 11,000 tonnes of freight passed through the airport in the year 2000, an increase of 2,000 tonnes from 1999.

Three specialist cargo companies are currently based at Cork Airport serving the European markets daily. These are DHL, TNT and UPS.

- - -

Both the Irish Air Corps and the Royal Air Force / Royal Naval Air Stations have contributed greatly in terms of assistance with search and rescue activities off the south and southwest coast over the years and their work is greatly appreciated at Cork Airport.

## The Irish Air Corps .

Although the Air Corps has never had any of its aircraft based at the Cork Airport, still many of them visit in the course of their military missions. Indeed, the record shows that the first official arrival was a Dove from Baldonnel, and

An Air Corps Aloutte 3 Helicopter at Cork Airport, 18th April 1999. They have often visited there or at the University Hospital on rescue or ambulance missions.
*Photo – Gabriel Desmond*

264

since that time it is safe to assume that every single Air Corps aircraft has landed there at one time or another.

Alouette helicopters are still very useful in their important air ambulance role, and when collecting patients in Cork city hospitals, will almost certainly refuel at the airport. For missions after dark, it is almost always a Dauphin that will perform these urgent tasks. Their ability to eliminate the long road journey to the specialist hospitals in Dublin has saved many lives over the years. In urgent medical cases time saved is invaluable. Naturally the Alouettes also carry Ministers or other officials as required to the Cork area, particularly if a new commercial development is involved, or if an event of national importance is taking place.

The young cadet pilots are introduced to the "peculiarities" of the airport's navigational aids at a relatively early stage of their career, when they fly their Marchetti trainers down from Baldonnel. En route, they gain valuable airways flying experience, while in the terminal area they get to fly down the instrument landing system, always to a successful landing, and sometimes for a short tea break! At certain times of the year, it would not be unusual to have up to four different Marchettis arriving at the airport in a short space of time, no doubt to the delight of the local aviation enthusiasts.

Another green piston-engine type to visit Cork regularly is the Cessna 172 of Army Co-Op Squadron, based not at Baldonnel, but at Gormanston, Co. Meath. This veteran is used for cash escort duties, providing top cover for the many cash-carrying armoured vans that are escorted throughout the country by both army and Garda personnel. Occasionally, the Cessna will land at the airport and collect local military personnel who may wish to monitor opera-

One of two Spanish 235 maritime patrol aircraft acquired by the Irish Air Corps in December 1994,seen here at Cork Airport 3rd January. 1995.

*Photo – Gabriel Desmond*

tions from the air, later dropping back to allow them return to Collins Barracks.

The cancelled Air Spectacular of 1985 probably saw the greatest number of Irish military aircraft on the ground in Cork contemporaneously but they could not get aloft due to the fog, and a few were forced to return to Baldonnel without breaking cloud.

Just five years later, in July 1990, a smaller Air Corps armada did arrive successfully for an important maritime event. No less than five Fouga Magisters, comprising the Silver Swallows aerobatics team, led by Capt Kevin Barry, flew across from Shannon, where Air Spectacular 1990 had been held the previous day. Other arrivals included the Bae 125, a King Air, a couple of Cessnas; a Dauphin and an Alouette.

The Silver Swallows had been escorted from Shannon, via County Kerry, by a pair of Luftwaffe Tornadoes, which resulted in the complete formation of seven jets flying low over Cork city producing lots of noise. With a waggle of their variable-geometry wings the Germans blasted upwards towards the stratosphere and home, while the Fougas landed as planned. The maritime event was the official opening of the Sean Lemass Berth at Ringaskiddy, by Mrs Máirín Haughey, wife of the then Taoiseach. It was felt that an aerial salute by the five Fougas would be appropriate, as the liner QE2 was present especially for the day. All went well, thankfully, but the military crews could not help noticing that the latter carried its own Dauphin helicopter on the upper deck!

The current Ministerial Air Transport Service jet, the Gulfstream IV, visits Cork on missions and sometimes carries out training sorties away from the more crowded airspace near Dublin. Occasionally, a minister or other official may wish to be collected from Cork before flying on to a European

Union meeting, and if the GIV is unavailable the King Air will carry out the task. On rare occasions, the mission may involve a flight to the USA, in which case it is relatively simple for the GIV to depart Baldonnel, collect more passengers at Cork and then head out over the North Atlantic.

Since their delivery to Maritime Squadron in December 1994, the two CASA CN.235 maritime patrol aircraft have occasionally landed at Cork, usually to take on patrol a naval officer from Haulbowline, although sometimes the extra crew member may be an officer of the Customs Service. The CASA's national prominence rose a little in 1999, when, after the death of former Taoiseach Jack Lynch, one was used to carry his coffin from Baldonnel to his final resting place in Cork. Thousands saw the State ceremony on television, during which an army bearer party drawn from the Southern Brigade, carried the coffin from the rear ramp of the CASA and placed it on the gun carriage for the procession from Cork Airport to the church. It was fitting that Mr Lynch's last flight had been in an Air Corps aircraft.

It is not all certain what new types will be ordered to replace the Air Corps' ageing fleet, but it is surely a safe assumption that shortly after their delivery they will be flown down to Cork, so that the citizens of the second city will not feel left out!

# The Royal Air Force and The Royal Naval Air Search and Rescue Service.

The Royal Air Force has visited Cork many times over the years. The first occasion was the visit by an Avro Shackleton maritime patrol aircraft and two Whirlwind helicopters following the ditching of the Flying Tiger Constellation in

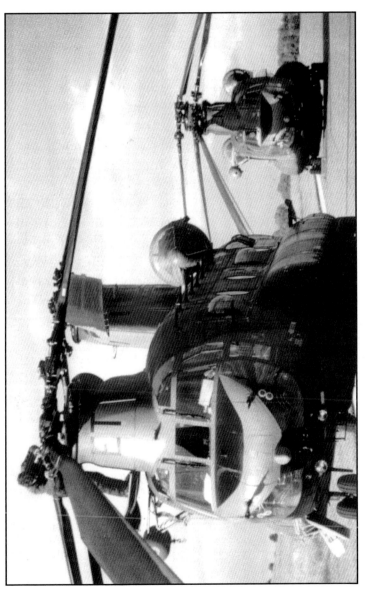

Two RAF Chinook Helicopters at Cork Airport 24th June 1985 during the Air India search and recovery operation. Here, one is being serviced during a lull in operations.

*Photo – Gabriel Desmond*

September 1962. Most RAF visits have been since 1983 when the bigger Sea King helicopters from 212 Sqdn. at RAF Brawdy in Wales began to appear.

In a typical operation, a RAF Sea King would transit from its base, refuel at Cork and then proceed out to sea to lift people from a ship or from the water, up to 200 miles off Ireland, maybe at night, in storm conditions. It would then return to land, often directly with survivors to The Cork University Hospital and Cork Airport. In extreme cases, it would leave all non-essential items at Cork, to maximise its payload and give it an endurance of over five hours.

The Chinook is the RAF's biggest helicopter with an endurance of up to eight hours. Chinooks came to Cork in 1985 for the Air India Recovery mission and in 1994 following the sinking of the ship Christianakis 250 miles off West Cork. Unfortunately, no survivors were found on those occasions but there have been many successful rescues. On the night of 23rd November 1986, two Sea Kings lifted 28 survivors from the ship Kowloon Bridge off the Mizen Head and landed them at Cork Airport. In February 1990, 10 people were airlifted to Cork from the ship Tribulus. On 4th January 1998, two RAF Sea Kings lifted 10 Spanish trawler crewmen from a raft, which had been dropped by an RAF Nimrod.

The RAF use the Bae 125 business jet for VIP transport. One brought the British Foreign Secretary, Douglas Hurd, to Cork in May 1990 for an EC Council of Ministers meeting at Parknasilla. Another Bae 125 visited in June 1994 in support of a helicopter rescue mission.

The Royal Naval Air Search and Rescue Service has also been associated with Cork Airport since it opened in 1961. As well as refuelling at the airport during numerous marine

A Sea King Helicopter of the Royal Naval 771 Air Squadron based at Culdrose, Cornwall, at Cork Airport 15th June 1994. It had come to support another Sea King that had developed a fuel leak after attending a ship 250 miles off the west coast of Ireland.

*Photo – Gabriel Desmond*

search and rescue missions off the south and south west coast of Ireland, it has played a major role on occasions when the airport was designated the rescue centre. Chief among these was the Air India Disaster in 1985, when numerous bodies were recovered from the sea. The 771 Naval Air Squadron at Culdrose, Cornwall provides that kind of assistance, when called upon.

The Squadron was first formed in 1939 at Lee on Solent as a Fleet Requirements Unit flying various types of fixed wing aircraft. In 1945 it received the Hoverfly helicopter, making it the first Royal Navy Squadron to operate helicopters. It disbanded in 1947 as part of defence reductions following World War II but was reformed in 1961 at RNAS Portland as a helicopter trials squadron for Whirlwind and Wasp helicopters.

771 Squadron moved to its present home at RNAS Culdrose in 1974. Today, it is specifically dedicated to civil and military Search and Rescue (SAR). The Westland Sea King Mk V helicopters, with their more powerful engines, longer range and improved avionics, which they used since 1988, have enabled the Squadron to assume a long range day/night all weather Search and Rescue capability. In most cases, crews are airborne within 5 minutes of being scrambled. The Squadron averages over 220 SAR missions a year, ranging from responding to distress calls along the Cornish coast to long range rescues in the Southwest Approaches.

The 771 crews have often been cited for exceptional skill and bravery during challenging rescues in very poor weather conditions. Recent awards included The Guild of Air Pilots and Air Navigators, Prince Philip Helicopter Rescue Award 1996 and the Shipwrecked Fishermen and Mariner's

President Karl Karstens of the Germany Federal Republic, who had been on a State visit to Ireland, seen here second from left on 1st May 1980, prior to his departure from Cork Airport. Also in picture is President Patrick Hillery and Barra O Tuama Aer Rianta Director. On extreme left is Jim Corr Lord Mayor of Cork.

*Photo – Courtesy Irish Examiner*

Royal Benevolent Society's Edward & Masie Lewis Award for 1996/1997.

The Squadron's distinctive Red and Grey livery of its aircraft is a familiar sight at Cork Airport during times of aviation or marine distress off the south and southwest coast.

## Famous Personalities

An airport by its very nature acts as a focal point for the arrival or departure of many well-known personalities in all walks of life, politicians, stars of stage and screen, athletes, rock stars etc. Over the years, Cork Airport has had its share of them. Most Irish politicians passed through the airport at one time or another as well as some foreign ones and a goodly sprinkle of foreign heads of state on private or official visits.

Those who came include two Presidents of the Federal Republic of Germany, Heindrich Lübke (1968) and Karl Carstens (1980). Other visitors have included General de Gaulle of France (1969), President Francois Mitterand of France (1988), President Nyerere of Tanzania (1979), Pres. Mario Soares of Portugal (1993), President Chiluba of Zambia (1995) President Yoweri Kaguta Musevani of Uganda (2000) and King Carl Gustav of Sweden (1992).

Among the celebrities past and present that came were Jack Doyle (1972); Johnny Cash (1985); Russell Harty (1985); Michael Jackson (1988); Show Jumper Harvey Smith (1992; Barbara Knox - 'Rita' in Coronation Street (1993); Boxer Chris Eubank (1995); Liverpool Footballer Robbie Fowler (1996); Mother Theresa of Calcutta (1996); David Essex (1997); Footballer Paul McGrath (1998); Bishop Tutu of South Africa

International singer Ella Fitzgerald arriving at Cork Airport for Cork
Jazz Festival in 1980 accompanied by Festival PRO Pearse Harney.
*Photo – Cork Jazz Festival Committee*

(1998); The Danish Prince Joachim and Princess Alexandra (Oct. 1998). Sarah, Duchess of York was a regular visitor.

Charlie Chaplin, Fred Astaire, Peter Ustinov, Sean Connery, Lawrence Harvey and Liam Neeson were among the film actors who passed through the airport. Charlotte Rampling came when scenes for her film, The Purple Taxi, were shot at the airport as did Lesley Anne Down, when scenes from the film The Great Train Robbery were shot at Kent Railway Station.

Music Festivals in Cork or at other southern venues brought their quota of performers including Bono and U2, Don McLean and Demis Roussis. The Cork Guinness Jazz Festival since its inception in 1978 brought some of the great names in that music to Cork Airport including Ronnie Scott, Cleo Lane, Johnny Dankworth, Ella Fitzgerald, Oscar Peterson and Stefan Grapelli.

The world of Athletics brought its own heroes to the airport en route to the Cork City Sports including the great Rhono, Steve Ovett, Steve Cramm, John Walker and of course Cobh Olympic Silver Medallist, Sonia O'Sullivan.

Jack Charlton, former manager of the Republic of Ireland soccer team arrived on a few occasions. There is a life size sculpture of him in fishing gear in the airport terminal building, beside the fish pond on the ground floor.

Cork Airport has been host to many famous men and women including Neil Armstrong in 1979, the first man to walk on the moon. They make up but a tiny fraction of those who passed through on business or pleasure during the last forty years.

Paddy Cole, well known jazz musician points to his photograph among those of many performing artists on exhibition at Cork Airport during the Guinness Jazz festival in 2000.
*Photo – Aer Rianta Cork*

Sonia O'Sullivan arriving at Cork Airport following her Silver Medal
victory in the Sydney 2000 Olympics.
*Photo – Courtesy Jim Hurley*

# Taxi Driver of the Year Award

Since 1986, the annual award by Aer Rianta is given to a taxi man from the Cork Airport group who has shown special merit based on the following criteria:-

1. Courtesy and quality of service provided, i.e. clean vehicle etc.

2. Useful knowledge of the Airport and Region which is of benefit to customers i.e. information concerning flights, accommodation availability, entertainment, special events, tourist attractions and commercial activities.

3. Commendation by members of the travelling public and airport staff during the year.

Winners have been:-Tony O'Riordan (1986), Mick Lucey (1987), Paddy O'Mahony (1988), Eamon Stapleton (1989), Peter Kearney (1990), Tom Looney (1991), Tony Hornibrook (1992), Finbar Gurhy (1993). Declan O'Callaghan (1994), Derry Coughlan (1995), Pat O'Riordan (1996), Paddy Hussey (1997), Eddy O'Sullivan (1998), Derry Williamson (1999), Frank Kennedy (2000).

# CULTURAL AND SPORTING ACTIVITIES

Over the years, various cultural and sporting activities were prominent at the airport.   Some are still active, others have died away.

# Racing & Coursing

Since 1987, Aer Rianta have sponsored the Clonmel Race Meeting held on 1st November each year. They also sponsor

Denis Maher, Duty Manager, presenting the Cork Airport Taxi Driver of the Year Award to Tony Hornibrook in Dec. 1993. On right is Barry Roche, Airport General Manager.

*Photo – Aer Rianta Cork*

Having a good time at Clonmel Races 1st Nov. 2000. L to R:- Lilibeth Horne, Commercial Manager Cork Airport, Jim Clifford (ex Immigration), Sheila Murphy Deputy General Manager Cork Airport.

*Photo – Courtesy Runway Magazine*

the Munster Oaks Greyhound Classic at Waterford Stadium and Millstreet Horse Show since 1990.

## Aer Lingus Golfing Society

There are currently two Golfing Societies at the airport, i.e. Cork Airport Golfing Society and Aer Lingus Golfing Society. The former has been active since the early 1960s and the latter operated as a society within a society. The reason for this is that all the Aer Lingus golfers participated in the Airport Golfing Society but travelled abroad as Aer Lingus Society and competed as such in all inter-Airline competitions.

Nowadays, both societies operate independently but many members of Aer Lingus have dual membership. The earliest records available of the Airport Society are from 1965. The subscription list for that year contains the following names: G. Holohan, P. Bracken, T. Bradley, D. Cahill, A. Davis, D. Murray, J. Harrington, P. Herlihy, B. Foley, J. Ward, B. Clancy, M. Mallon. Each is recorded as paying five shillings, equivalent to 25p, annual sub. The first competition recorded was held at Douglas G. C. on 1st July 1965. Eight of the above list contributed and paid five shillings as fees for the day. The princely sum of two pounds ten shillings was spent on one dozen golf balls as prizes for the day. The winner is not recorded.

The Aer Lingus Golfing Society now has almost forty members, both male and female. In 2000, the Society won the Aer Lingus Inter-Regional Golf Championship on home soil at Kinsale G. C. and will defend the title this year at Faithlegg G. C., Co. Waterford. Through this competition, the Aer Lingus Society has played many wonderful courses over the years, at home and abroad, the Black G.C. (Bethpage NY),

Turning the sod on 25th January 2000 for the building of the Cork Airport Great Southern Hotel. In the cab of the JCB – Noel Hanlon, Chairman Aer Rianta; Mary O'Rourke T.D. Minister for Public Enterprise. Standing L to R:- Joe O'Connor, General Manager Cork Airport; John Burke, Chie Exec. Aer Rianta; Eamon McKeown, Chief Exec. Great Southern Hotels; Michael Daly of P.J. Hegarty & Sons, Main Building Contractors.

*Photo – Courtesy Runway Magazine*

Foxhills (London), Lahinch, Rosses Point, Waterloo (Brussels), Tamiment N.J. being just a few.

## Cork Airport Golfing Society (C.A.G.S.)

Founded in the early days of the airport, when a leisurely pace and time for a chat were all important, the Cork Airport Golfing Society has been the catalyst for many a good yarn and many loving friendships.

Playing golf at that time was mainly for those in senior management positions and very few of the ordinary staff was involved. The founders of the Society could not have realised that many years later it still provides a social outlet for people employed at the airport.

The early days saw a few playing and the outings were mainly confined to Golf Clubs within easy reach of the airport. Improving transport facilities allowed the members to be more adventurous and courses in distant and not too distant places became accessible. Weekends away became and still are a very important item on the golfing calendar. Places such as Waterville, Ceann Sibeal in Dingle and Mount Juliet feature regularly while Spain, USA, UK and France have all featured in the social calendar of the C.A.G.S.

The Aer Rianta Quadrangular is a yearly competition for staff from Cork, Dublin, Shannon together with staff from the Great Southern Hotels Group. The Cork Society has enjoyed its share of success in this competition. The Society has been involved in fundraising for different charities and has raised over £10,000 for Aid Cancer Treatment (A.C.T.), which is based at the Cork University Hospital.

Cork Airport Golfing Society has, like all such societies, seen many changes in its personnel. Members come and go but the Society still brings together staff from all departments at the airport. Indeed, many people who have now retired are still playing and enjoying the social cut and thrust that are still a feature of the gatherings of the Airport Golf Society.

## Cork Airport Angling Club.

The Cork Airport Angling Club, which came into being in 1977 had among its   founding members Niall Birmingham, (R.I.P.) Mick O'Reilly, John O'Regan, Tomas O Beara, Peter O'Neill, John Beard and Billy McCarthy. Originally the main interest was in trout fishing and some very enjoyable days were spent on the Lee, the Bandon, and the Sulane. But trout fishing could often mean spending long tiresome days on the riverbank with little or no results and unless one is a seasoned angler it can become a very tedious and boring occupation. It was suggested that a few sea outings be arranged and from then on sea angling became the main activity of the group.

The Aer Lingus two-day International Sea Angling Competition was an annual event held in Cork since 1975 and it was the ambition of Cork Airport Angling Club members to enter a team for the event in 1979. Their application was turned down, as they did not represent an airline. They were, however, permitted, to take part in the outing but not in the competition. The following year, a team was again submitted for the event but this time under "Aer Lingus, Cork". The application was accepted and they felt they had really joined the elite when they captured the Aer Lingus International Trophy, (the first Irish team to do so), the Dessie Desmond Perpetual Trophy for the best Irish team and the Best Individual Overall event (Billy Joyce). The team mem-

After a Sea Angling Trip to Kinsale in 1982 Niall Bermingham, Joe Pey, Mick O'Reilly, Tony Kenneally.
*Photo – Courtesy Joe Pey*

bers were: Mick O'Reilly (captain) Niall Birmingham, Billy Joyce and Billy McCarthy.

Then came the Messiah from the midlands in the person of a young lad called Joe Pey, who had a great flair for organisation. He was immediately elected to the office of chairman, secretary, registrar and any other position available. From then on outings were organised, seven dates were agreed annually and boats were hired. While outings were great fun events, a friendly rivalry developed between members, and so was born the "A" team and the "B" team. Since then many members have come and gone but there is still a core group involved whose intention is to relive the glory days of the Cork Airport Angling Club in the years ahead.

## Aer Lingus Soccer Team

Although a soccer team was formed at the airport shortly after it opened, the Aer Lingus Soccer Club wasn't officially formed until 1965. A team was entered that year in the Cork and District Shipping League, the city's inter-firm soccer competitions. Success did not come until 1976 when the team defeated Marina Bakeries in a play off to win the 2nd Div. Championship and gained promotion.

It took 8 years, a relegation back to the 2nd Division and a subsequent promotion before success returned to the Club. In 1984 the team were runners up to Postal Workers in the 1st Division and in the following year the Club won the 1st Divisional Championship for the first time. They were Premier Cup champions in 1988, Shield champions in 1990 and won the treble i.e. Premier League, Shield and Premier Cup in 1994. In 1996 they again won the Premier Cup and in 1997 the Premier Shield.

Aer Lingus AFC - Team who defeated Cambrian Airways 2-1 in Nov. 1974. Back Row L to R:- Tom Kerrigan, Barry Murphy, Jim Kearney, Patsy Dorgan, Ron Hyde, John Prendergast, Jerry Carroll, Eddy Hegarty, John Buckley. Front Row L to R:- Dan Scanlon, Noel Bradley, Mick O'Mahony, Jerry Lane, Jerry Crowley.

*Photo – Courtesy Noel Bradley*

288

Over the years the Club has travelled widely including New York, Atlanta, Frankfurt, Brussels, Amsterdam, Copenhagen, Paris, London, Cardiff, Finland and Zurich. In 1979 the Club was invited to take part in its first inter-airline tournament – The Golden Tulip Tournament in Amsterdam hosted by KLM. They came second in 1980, third in 1981 and also third in 1982. One of the greatest achievements of the Aer Lingus Soccer Club has been the formation of its own Inter-Airline Soccer Tournament in 1981 called the Aer Lingus Shamrock Tournament. Aer Lingus Cork was second in that competition in 1981 and won it in 1984. They also were third in the Midnight Sun Tournament (Finland) in 1982 and 4th in the European Airport Cup (Dublin) in 1984. The team also participated in the European Airports Tournament in Amsterdam, Malta and Rome. Aer Lingus AFC also hosted the Shamrock Tournament in Cork.

Aer Lingus AFC ceased playing in 1997 and Cork Airport AFC was formed in 1998. Similar successes are expected from the airport club in due course.

## Cork Airport Badminton Club

The Club was formed in 1972 and based in the Bristow Helicopter Hangar. In 1973 it moved to Greenmount School in Cork City. It was very successful and over the years was one of the largest in Cork covering grades Division 1 to Division 6. Many Club members competed at inter-county level. It was eventually disbanded in 1988.

# GAA at the Airport

In the early days following the opening of Cork Airport, a meeting was convened there and a club was formed called the Aer Lingus / Aer Rianta GAA Club. Since then, it has played an important part in the lives of the Airport staff. The club is now called The Cork Airport GAA Club.

At the outset, teams travelled to Kinsale to play the locals, every player trying his best but at the same time feeling there wasn't anything at stake. However things soon changed and in the true spirit of the GAA, it became very competitive. Kinsale players felt they were playing for the honour and glory of their club and even though the Airport Club was made up of those from many counties, it was felt that Cork Airport was now their new home, with which they could identify.

As time went on they became more adventurous and travelled overseas to London, Birmingham, New York, Boston and Rome. They also played in triangular tournaments with Dublin Shannon and Cork Airports, all fielding very strong teams. One such tournament in Shannon was so hotly contested that the referee had to call all players together and read the riot act to them. Memory recalls that Dublin beat Shannon in the final, which was a cracking game.

The club has had many successes winning Inter Firm Competitions in both hurling and football. The most recent win, the Murphy Cup, was in football in November 1999. One airport man who gave an example to everyone, both on and off the pitch, was the famous Jackie Daly of the Glen Rovers Club. For spirit, determination and ability, he had them in abundance.

Aer Lingus AFC – Winners of Cork & District Shipping League 2nd Division Title 1976. Back Row L to R:- Ron. Hyde, Patsy Dorgan, Noel Bradley, Owen McCarthy, Pat Harrington, Barry Murphy. Front Row L to R:- Donal Crowley, Mick O'Mahony, Jim Kearney (Capt.) Jerry Lane, Kevin Cannon, Liam Good.

*Photo – Courtesy Noel Bradley*

APF Jackie Daly, a former Glen Rovers hurling colleague of Christy Ring
pictured with the maestro's wife in front of his sculpture at Cork Airport.
*Photo – Courtesy Cáit Ward.*

A Cork Airport GAA football team who played Kinsale in 1962. Back Row L to R:- P. Dempsey, D. Harris, J. Murphy, D. Maher, M. Quinlan B. O'Connell, B. Roche, T. Kerrigan, K. Farrell, P. Gallagher, P. Doherty, D .Desmond. Front Row L to R:- D. Collins, R. Maloney, O. Kelly, V. Lane, T. Russell J. O'Donnell, M. McAuliffe.

*Photo – Courtesy Donie Harris*

# Cork Airport Singers.

The Cork Airport Singers were founded in September 1986 to participate in the celebration of the 25th anniversary of Cork Airport and throughout the years have been extremely active. The group, which were all airport employees, launched a recording in 1989 entitled "A Flight Around Munster with the Cork Airport Singers". In 1991, it was decided to open membership to persons outside Cork Airport and since then the choir has been growing in strength to its present membership of sixty-eight.

The choir participates in numerous concerts and fund raising events yearly and in the past eighteen months accompanied Finbar Wright in the Opera House, produced its own show to a full house in the Everyman Theatre and accompanied the Cork Youth Orchestra in the City Hall. They also participated in a Mass with Cardinal Cathal Daly in the North Cathedral, delighted audiences in Siamsa Tire in Tralee, sang live on the Marian Finnucane Christmas Show from Cork in December 2000 and appeared in many other shows.

The choir also takes part in choral festivals and competitions and in the recent past has been a successful competitor in Feis Maitiu and the Cork Choral Festival. In the New Ross Choral Festival in 2000, the choir was overjoyed to be awarded two first prizes in the senior choir competitions.

The present year 2001 shows the singers with many events entered in the diary but most important of all will be the production of a CD containing a selection of their favourite songs.

The choir's Musical Director is Ms Ann Healy Mayes, who has been with the group since its formation and is responsible for the level of professionalism achieved to date.

Cork Airport Singers celebrating 25th Anniversary Mass 16th October 1986

**Back Row** L to R:- J. Guiry, G. Ward, J. Drennan, P. Dorgan, G. Leonard, T. Maye, J. Carroll, J. O'Mahony, P. O'Connell, J. Daly. **4th Row** L to R:- G. Harrington, B. Lynch, M. Healy, K. Donovan, A. Sullivan, D. Scanlan, D. Foley, J. Lane, M. Ahern, N. Daly. **3rd Row** L to R:- M. O'Leary, S. Ryan, U. O'Reilly, E. Lenihan, R. Cahill, C. Cotter, P. Laffin, S. Kenneally, E. Culloty. **2nd Row** L to R:- E. O'Connor, U. Barry, E. Milner, S. Murphy, I. Falvey, M. Fleming M. Lynch, F. Hogan, D. Niblock.

**Front Row** L to R:- P. Gallagher, M. Costello, A. Healy, J. Harrington, Canon Cahalane.

*Photo - Courtesy Ray Shanahan*

295

# 7

# CHAPTER SEVEN

Cork International Airport, gateway to the South of Ireland, is easily accessible by air from Europe, the United States and the UK. Over 40 airlines provide regular scheduled and chartered services at the airport, which is only 8 km from Cork City. Waterford, Tipperary and Kilkenny are within easy reach via the new Jack Lynch Tunnel. A frequent bus service operates from the airport to the city centre and train services operate downtown from Kent station.

Cork Airport is the gateway to Ireland's finest scenery of West Cork and Killarney. There are over 100 golf courses close at hand including the world- renowned Old Head of Kinsale, Fota, Mount Juliet, Waterville and Ballybunion. Other leisure pursuits in Cork, Kerry and Waterford include deep-sea angling, sailing and equestrian sports. The gourmet capital of Ireland, Kinsale, always provides an unforgettable dining experience. The University City of Cork offers unique heritage centres such as Blarney Castle and the City Gaol. Only an hour's journey takes one to the historic Rock of Cashel in Tipperary, the world famous Waterford crystal factory and the wonderful Lismore Castle Estate.

Even though it took 35 years for the airport to reach the magic figure of one million passengers a year, it has been a major success story. When it opened in October 1961, 90 people were employed, today employment is in excess of 1000

Photo taken at Cork Airport in June 2000 when Dermot Collins, Chairman of Kinsale UDC and a former member of Cork APFS made a courtesy visit there. Standing L to R:- Miah Keohane, John Smyth, Máirín Ahern, Liam O'Shea, Morogh Mc Hugh, Lilibet Horne, Donal Crowley, Kevin Farrell. Seated L to R:- Mick Staunton, Sean O'Connell, Joe O'Connor Airport General Manager, Dermot Collins, Donal Barrett, Asst. Co. Manager, Ray Dwane, Kinsale Town Clerk.

*Photo – Tony O'Connell Photography*

and 1300 are employed in the Airport Business Park. In the first full year of operation, the airport handled over 77,000 passengers. At the end of the year 2000 the figure was 1,680,160 and at the end of this year, 2001, it is expected that the figure will have reached 1.8 million. A forecast of 2.5 million passengers has been made for 2005.

## Privatisation of Cork Airport

In 1999 there was much publicity both in the press and media that moves were afoot by the Government to have the airports privatised. This was of particular concern to staff at Cork Airport at a time when Aer Rianta was due to announce a £61m plan for a five-year development of the airport. A lobby group was formed called Cork Airport Against Break-up (C.A.A.B.) under the chairmanship of Donal Harris (Airport Police/Fire Service) to campaign against selling off the airport to a private consortium. The group lobbied support from T.Ds, Councillors, Cork Corporation, Cork Co. Council, Cork Chambers of Commerce, Cork Council of Trade Unions, I.B.E.C., Government Ministers and other groups or bodies with an interest in Cork Airport's future. C.A.A.B. has been very effective and responsible in its approach.

Aviation is expanding rapidly and airports cannot stand still. Huge sums of money are required for the development and expansion of the three international airports, Dublin, Shannon and Cork. The Minister for Public Enterprise Mary O'Rourke and Minister for Finance Charlie McCreevey commissioned a report on the future strategic direction of Aer Rianta. In the report by Warburg Dillon Read, most of the main points highlighted by them were in line with Aer

These six youthful looking lads hold the record of having worked at Cork Airport on opening day and are still employed there today. L to R:- Tom Russell, Michael Healy, Denis Maher, Donie Harris Pat Gallagher, Michael Staunton.

*Photo – Aer Rianta Cork.*

Rianta's own analysis. Chief among them was the consultants' recommendation that Aer Rianta be floated on the Stock Market through an Initial Public Offering (IPO).

Mr John Burke, Chief Executive of Aer Rianta writing in Runway magazine about the future direction of Aer Rianta had this to say:

"Aer Rianta has a very clear strategy, which is to continue owning and developing the three airports in Ireland and to expand overseas in our core business of airport management and airport retailing.... Funding the strategy is the key issue. At Dublin, Cork and Shannon Airports, we need to be spending in excess of £100m each year to cater for the growth in passenger numbers. We have also major opportunities overseas for which funding would be required. Our current level of profit - £31m is too low to meet these funding requirements and we cannot meet the shortfall from borrowings alone, which are now growing quite sharply.

Government policy is not to provide funding for Aer Rianta, or indeed any semi-state company, so we need funding from sources outside the company. This can be achieved in two ways – either by selling part of the company or floating a minority of our shares on the stock market through an IPO (Initial Public Offering). We see an IPO as the best way of funding the business strategy and meeting the needs of all the stakeholders, including shareholders, customers and employees. Other airports have been floated in this way and a significant number are moving in the same direction."

## THE FUTURE by Joe O'Connor, Cork Airport's General Manager.

"The forty years of Cork Airport's existence could be summarised as 30 years of slow steady progress followed by 10 hectic years during which passenger growth continually outstripped capacity despite investment of over £30 million during the past decade.

Future decades are confidently expected to be positive and full of opportunity and excitement. Side by side with the economic success of the whole country, Cork Airport is forecast to double passenger numbers by 2010 and to grow to a 5 million-passenger airport by 2020.

The immediate challenge is to get the infrastructural development in place as quickly as possible. Passenger traffic through Cork Airport in the year 2000 reached 1.68 million. The current terminal facilities are designed to accommodate 1.1 million. This has resulted in overcrowding at peak times and an unacceptable standard of comfort for passengers.

In 1999, it was accepted that the rate of growth called for urgent action. Based upon a master plan, which had recently been completed, a development plan was prepared. It took a more long-term view than ever before because of the growth forecast. The realisation that any new construction would be a forerunner of further phases of expansion influenced the planning process.

A long-term concept was developed which took account of a 5 million passenger throughput in approximately 20 years time. Then a detailed plan for a 2.5 million passenger airport was drawn up and this is what is being built at present. It includes a pier building and 3 Air-Bridges as well as

Hold Baggage Screening facilities, which are a mandatory requirement as from 1st January 2003. The estimated cost of the Terminal Development is close to £50 million.

In addition to the Terminal expansion, other works include a major apron extension and a new taxiway connecting the end of the runway to the apron. An £8 million contract is 50% completed and will be fully so in 2002. This will provide a designated wide-bodied aircraft stand as well as more stands for general use.

Another £18 million project includes road improvements, a new roundabout at the entrance to the Business Park and a major investment in car park facilities including a 600 space multi-storey car park with a covered walkway connection to the Terminal.

Other investments include £2.5 million on a major upgrade of the Fire Station and £5 million on airfield and environmental improvements. It is expected that a minimum of £10 million will be spent each year for the next 10 years in Capital Development.

As part of the long term plan for Cork Airport, a Land Use Study was carried out in 1996 which dealt with four main areas of consideration:- airfield; passenger terminal site; a new site south of runway 07/25 and a remote site west of runway 17/35.

Airfield: This area covers the lands, which will be required for airfield developments to meet future demand and include (a) provision for extension to both runways; (b) provision of additional aircraft parking; (c) provision of a parallel taxiway for the main runway.

Passenger Terminal Site: This area currently contains almost all the facilities of Cork Airport including the Passenger Terminal. It is proposed to make use of this site primarily for passenger processing with the transfer of other facilities to new locations. On the basis of current traffic trends, it is anticipated that passenger movements of over 5 million per annum can be accommodated on this site.

New Site South of Runway 07/25 – adjacent to Kinsale Road (40 acres):

Aer Rianta acquired this site in 1998 for future expansion. It is proposed that this site be used for the development of all non-passenger related services, which require both airside and road access such as cargo, aircraft maintenance, aircraft parking and ancillary facilities such as long term parking for both the public and car hire companies.

Remote Site – West of Runway 17/35: This site currently contains the fire training area and provides a suitable site for facilities which (a) do not require public access; (b) do require good access to all parts of the airfield; (c) would otherwise occupy prime sites in the zones for commercial development. Possible operations for this site include airfield maintenance facilities, fire station and control tower.

However, since that study was carried out, the Aer Rianta Board decided at the end of January 2001 to make the relocation of the Control Tower west of Runway 17/35 a short term project instead of a long term one and so create a new Air Traffic Control centre in that area. The decision to relocate, as soon as possible, was influenced by the complexity and cost of refurbishing the existing building and was the preferred choice of The Irish Aviation Authority.

Reverting again to the short term plan, the advent of the Commission for Aviation Regulation means that airport charges will be related to true costs and that they will be increased in a structured and transparent manner. Increased charges will be necessary to pay for the investment in new facilities.

Other issues include the future ownership of Aer Rianta. The company has a strategic plan, which envisages an IPO (Initial Private Offering) - partial privatisation. This would raise finance for investment in the airports while ensuring the continuing discipline of the stock market and permitting ongoing government control over an essential national infra-structural asset.

The whole aviation environment is entering a new phase of change, which has huge implications for airports. Aer Lingus, for example, have joined the One World Alliance. This could have big implications, especially for smaller airports like Cork.

Airports similarly are consolidating and it is hoped that Aer Rianta will become a major force in the business of Global Airport Alliances. Such a development would offer great backing to Cork Airport in the future.

A new Cork Airport Consultative Committee was estab-lished last year. It will ensure an informed political interest in the airport.

We are living in an age where the aviation industry is experiencing unprecedented change, expansion and devel-opment. Cork Airport is at the centre of all this and both management and staff are poised to meet all the challenges that are presented to them with the same determination as they have done during the past forty years.

Significant numbers of new staff have been recruited in recent years. It is confidently expected that these staff will use modern techniques and, combined with the best tradi-tions of service, which have been the hallmark of Cork

Airport, will ensure that the airport goes forward with confidence."

## Great Southern Hotel Cork Airport

The sod turning ceremony for the Cork Airport Great Southern Hotel was performed on 25th January 2000. In attendance were the Minister for Public Enterprise Mary O'Rourke; Aer Rianta and Great Southern Hotels' Chairman Noel Hanlon; Aer Rianta Chief Executive John Burke; General Manager Cork Airport Joe O'Connor; Great Southern Hotels' Chief Executive Eamonn McKeon and Michael Daly, P.J. Hegarty & Sons Ltd. main Contractors for the hotel.

Designed by Aer Rianta Technical Architects, it opened for business on 20th March 2001 under General Manager Pat Cussen and was officially opened by the Minister for Public Enterprise, Mary O'Rourke T.D. on 31st May. The contract for the interior design of the hotel was by RPW of London. Their brief, one of the design team, Aidan Healy, informed Runway magazine, was "to move slightly away from the branding of other hotels in the group. Our interpretation was that it should be a warm balanced, comfortable space to be in. It should offer different details but not in a fussy way – we wanted to get away from heavy colours and heavy fabrics. Most modern business people want to use hotels to make them relax and invite them to leave their work behind." The Sales Manager of Great Southern Hotels, Ms Catherine Cronin summed it up very well when she wrote:

"The new Great Southern Hotel Cork Airport has a very contemporary feel. Its interiors are spacious and modern with bright colours and lots of light. Its 81 Executive rooms come equipped with every facility the discerning traveller needs – mini bar, fax/modem connection, iron/trouser press, and interactive TV system featuring latest movie releases. Following in the traditions established by its sister hotels at Dublin and Shannon Airports, the aim is to establish a haven for the busy traveller, close to the airport, yet away from it. A 24 hour shuttle bus will run up to the terminal and a courtesy telephone in the Arrivals Hall will allow guests call the hotel when they arrive. Although a modern and contemporary hotel, the welcome is distinctly Irish."

Referring to the Hotel during its construction, Cork Airport General Manager Joe O'Connor said in Runway Magazine "It will certainly strengthen our position in attracting new business to the airport and in better serving our existing customers. Our product is vastly more marketable with the hotel on our doorstep.

## Cork Airport Business Park

The Business Park commenced in October 1998 on 45 acres close to the airport terminal. The cost of its construction is £80m and it is a partnership between Aer Rianta and ICC Bank. The 480,000 sq. ft. facility is one of only two digital commerce parks in Ireland and when fully operational will provide up to 2500/3000 jobs.

The Target Markets of the Business Park are Corporate Headquarters; Mobile Overseas Projects; spin-off from Pharmaceutical Companies in the Region; Leading edge/growth Companies in Software and IT Sectors; Campus Companies/R&D Facilities.

The Companies in the Business Park to date are as follows:-

Analog Devices, Atco Ireland, Avery Dennison, Black & Decker, Citco Data Processing, Com 21, Comdisco, Comnitel Technologies Ltd. Eirx Therapeutics, Fisher Rosemount Ireland, Garwyn, G.T.S., Hibernian Group, I.D.C., IMTF Software Ltd., Logica, Matrox, McKesson HBOC, Motorola, PM Centrix, Pfizers, Stocker Yale, Syskoplan Ltd., T.T.I. Ltd., UCC – Prosper Centre/Opera Centre/Minerva, V.E.C., Vistech.

In mid June 2001, employment in the Business Park was in excess of 1300 people. It will undoubtedly complement the Hotel development in contributing to the new dynamism of Cork Airport.

# COMMERCIAL PASSENGER FIGURES AT CORK AIRPORT
## 1961- 2000

| Year | Departures | Arrivals | Transit | Total |
|------|-----------|----------|---------|-------|
| 1961 | 4805 | 5231 | 136 | 10172 |
| 1962 | 36382 | 36245 | 3548 | 76184 |
| 1963 | 45504 | 45920 | 3831 | 95255 |
| 1964 | 53778 | 53887 | 5030 | 112695 |
| 1965 | 64598 | 64353 | 6466 | 135417 |
| 1966 | 76444 | 75392 | 7999 | 160135 |
| 1967 | 81035 | 78352 | 7869 | 167256 |
| 1968 | 77119 | 76794 | 8585 | 162498 |
| 1969 | 80969 | 77897 | 11478 | 172344 |
| 1970 | 92997 | 91463 | 13269 | 197729 |
| 1971 | 106652 | 104115 | 14182 | 224349 |
| 1972 | 103004 | 100885 | 13047 | 216936 |
| 1973 | 112403 | 110535 | 12775 | 235715 |
| 1974 | 116915 | 114878 | 12572 | 244365 |
| 1975 | 121937 | 119937 | 12626 | 254500 |
| 1976 | 131548 | 128459 | 11333 | 271340 |
| 1977 | 144925 | 140882 | 13179 | 298986 |
| 1978 | 162004 | 161929 | 10438 | 334371 |
| 1979 | 173153 | 169135 | 6250 | 348538 |
| 1980 | 157069 | 150371 | 5528 | 312968 |
| 1981 | 158779 | 54045 | 6741 | 319565 |
| 1982 | 156067 | 151615 | 6645 | 314327 |
| 1983 | 157765 | 155249 | 9831 | 322845 |
| 1984 | 161972 | 160229 | 10845 | 333046 |
| 1985 | 167216 | 163681 | 9799 | 340396 |
| 1986 | 175945 | 172340 | 8312 | 356597 |
| 1987 | 217001 | 214469 | 9038 | 440518 |
| 1988 | 262471 | 268021 | 11032 | 541524 |
| 1989 | 304491 | 310381 | 13770 | 628242 |
| 1990 | 336030 | 343397 | 28779 | 708206 |
| 1991 | 318607 | 320628 | 5711 | 664946 |

| 1992 | 343225 | 344109 | 4772  | 692106  |
|------|--------|--------|-------|---------|
| 1993 | 354940 | 358777 | 9448  | 723161  |
| 1994 | 395361 | 399434 | 5393  | 800188  |
| 1995 | 478588 | 484211 | 8520  | 971319  |
| 1996 | 551019 | 559512 | 13789 | 1124320 |
| 1997 | 586569 | 594201 | 15491 | 1196261 |
| 1998 | 645232 | 654859 | 15133 | 1315224 |
| 1999 | 738977 | 742961 | 19967 | 1501805 |
| 2000 | 836589 | 826001 | 17570 | 1680160 |

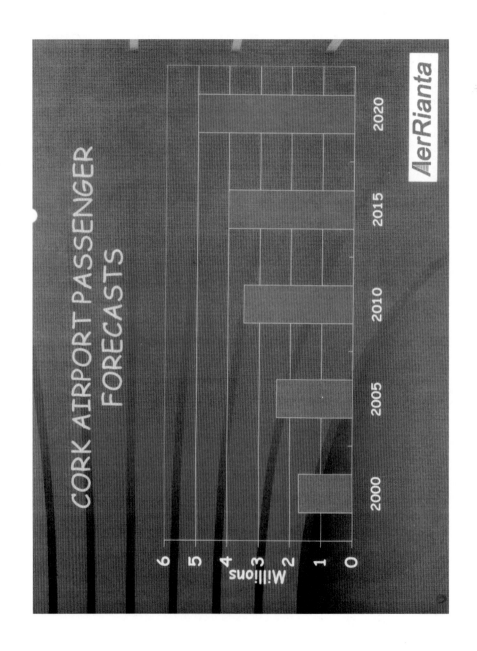

CORK AIRPORT PASSENGER FORECASTS

AerRianta

Passenger Numbers

311

# CHRONOLOGICAL LIST OF EVENTS

1928    First move to get an air base for Cork - Cork Harbour Commissioners invited Col. Charles Russell, former Irish Army Corps to address them.

1930    Beginning of decade saw trans-Atlantic seaplane service become a reality.

1933    Richard F. O'Connor, Cork Co. Surveyor makes his ideas for an airport known – aerodrome site at Belvelly and sea plane base in Cork Harbour; Cobham's Air Circus at Ballincollig 5th and 6th July.

1934    Branch of the Irish Aero Club formed in Cork in April.

1936    Foynes selected as sea-plane base; Site at Ahanesk, Midleton  chosen as site for a Cork airport following survey.

1939    Government approved proposal to establish a land airport for Cork -    World War II breaks out in September and all airport plans abandoned.

1943    Due rapid developments in aviation, Government requests further survey of potential airport sites. Ahanesk and Ballygarvan now the two main site contenders.

1948    Farmers Cross airfield officially opened Sun. 9th May.

1957    Government agrees in principle that the Cork airport should be built at Ballygarvan.

1959    Tenders invited for construction of airport – estimated cost £1m.

1961    Proving flights by Aer Lingus and Cambrian Airways carried out 12th    October. Airport officially opened 16th October.

1962    Great Southern Hotels appointed caterers at airport in Spring of 1962.  A Super Constellation ditched in Atlantic 23rd Sept. – Cork airport involved in search & rescue operations.

1963    Aer Lingus began operating an air car ferry on Cork-Bristol route using ATL-98 Carvairs (converted DC-4s)

1964    Harrington's took over airport catering from Great Southern Hotels; Flying club house officially opened 29th March; First jet to land at Cork Airport, a BOAC Comet G-APDI operated for Aer Lingus, on 31st July; British Eagle takes over Cork-Liverpool route from Starways; Guinness Festival Clock on display at airport June/July; Fatal crash of private plane, a five-seater Piper Comanche on 7th August – three members of the Gaulle family from Youghal and the pilot were killed.

1965    Cork-Manchester service inaugurated by Aer Lingus 31st May;Arrivals hall in terminal building widened; Control Tower double glazed; VASI (Visual Slope Indicator) lights installed on Runway 25; World War II planes at airport in June for the making of film The Blue Max; Douglas Bader, famous World War II RAF Fighter Pilot at airport 16th September and made honorary life member of Munster Aero Club.

1966    Pres. De Valera at airport 24th July en route to Cape Clear to open Irish College; Remains of Sister Eamon Sullivan, who was expelled by the Cultural Revolutionary Guards in Peking, landed in Cork.

1968    Outbreak of Foot & Mouth in UK - big effect on passenger figures in the first half of the year; Cork Airport management functions vested in Aer Rianta from Dept. of Transport & Power on 1st April; Aer Lingus Viscount St. Phelim EI-AOM crashed near Tuskar Rock Sun. 24th March – all on board killed; Charlie Chaplin and wife Oonagh at the airport in April;   First scheduled all night opening 1st June; President Lübke of German Federal Republic & his wife landed 5th June; British Eagle ceased operating on Cork-Liverpool route in November and went into bankruptcy.

1969    Charles de Gaulle landed at airport en route to Heron Cove Hotel near Parknasilla.

1970   Early 1970s Irish Helicopters began operations from Cork Airport; Transfer of State staff to Aer Rianta began; Three Aer Lingus Boeing 707s from Boston, New York and Chicago landed at Cork Airport 27th August due adverse weather at Dublin and Shannon.

1971   Bank of Ireland replaced Ulster Bank at the airport.

1972   First major development under Aer Rianta management – Fire Station extended; Airport water supply extended, new reservoir and piping installed; Duty Free shop commenced operations 8th Sept.

1973   VASI Lights installed on main runway 17/35; Airport Manager Paddy O'Grady transferred to Dublin in Sept. He was replaced by Gerry Holohan as Manager; Cork Airport rescue centre for the recovery of the Pisces III Mini-Submarine at the end of August.

1974   Gale force winds gusting up to 112 mph did considerable damage at airport – doors of Irish Helicopters Ltd. hangar were blown in – Joyce Aviation hangar wrecked and several planes destroyed.

1975   Aer Rianta undertook a passenger terminal study aimed at improving the terminal facilities. The findings resulted in the provision, over the next couple of years, of new departure and arrival halls, new check-in area and office complex, new information desk and duty office and new VIP

Lounge; Brymon Airways began operations from Plymouth to Cork.

1976    British Airways commenced scheduled services on the Cork/London route formerly operated by Cambrian Airways.

1977    New Duty Free Shop opened 18th December; Dan Air inaugural flight Cardiff/Bristol/Cork on 6th April.

1978    Completed extensions and facilities officially opened by the Taoiseach Jack Lynch T.D.; Members of Dutch royal family arrived at airport 1st July en route to Sneem, Co. Kerry.

1979    Whiddy Island Disaster 7th January – Cork Airport refuelling centre for Air Corps, Royal Navy and Irish Helicopters involved in the search and rescue; Tax Free Shop opened in February; Pres. Julius Nyerere o Tanzania at airport on 19th Sept. while on a state visit to Ireland.

1980    Main apron extended; Erection of first phase of security fence; Renovations carried out to Cargo Terminal and a new in-flight Catering Kitchen built; Pres. of German Federal Republic, Karl Karstens and his wife left Cork Airport for Germany 1st May following a three day official visit to Ireland; National strike of Aer Lingus mechanics took place 30th May – strike ended 4th July; Albert Reynolds, T.D. Minister for Transport on official visit 5th June.

1981   Inaugural Dan Air Cork-London Gatwick service 13th April; West German Chancellor Willi Brandt arrived at airport 2nd June.

1982   Avair commenced commuter service between Cork and Dublin on 13th January; Facilities for disabled installed at airport; High Mast flood lighting of the apron completed.

1983   Main car park enlarged; Mortuary provided; Cork Airport operations centre for secret rescue of seaman carried out from US Nuclear Submarine 6th July.

1984   Aer Lingus took over commuter service to Dublin; Gerry Holohan retired as Airport Manager in March and was replaced by Barry Roche; Airport Penthouse upgraded and its accommodation converted to offices etc.

1985   Installation of closed circuit television cameras on Control Tower enabling the entire airport area to be surveyed; due phenomenal increase in passenger traffic, Aer Rianta carried out survey of terminal with view to carrying out a major expansion and development programme; Air India disaster 23rd June – Cork Airport operations centre for search and rescue; Cork Air Spectacular cancelled in mid August due low cloud.

1986  Airport celebrated its 25th anniversary with an "open day".; Two highly sophisticated Instrument Landing Systems (ILS), one serving each end of the main runway were installed.

1987  Final phase of security fence around the airport completed; Accommodation in the Control Tower etc. restructured; Ryanair began operations at Cork on 8th June; Work began on extension of main runway in the autumn; In conjunction with this High Intensity Approach Lights and Centre Line Lighting were installed.

1988  Phase 1 of Terminal Expansion and Development Plan completed; Both Dublin and Cork Airports ceased to be forecast offices for Met Eireann - Shannon Airport became the Central Aviation Forecasting Office for the three State airports.

1989  Dan Air ended its operation of the Cork Gatwick route in March; Main Runway extension of 1000 feet opened 5th July by John Wilson T.D. Minister for Tourism and Transport; Iona Airways commenced pilot training school at the airport in May; European College of Aeronautics opened a similar establishment in September.

1990  Phase II of Terminal Expansion and Development Plan completed. Main ramp extension.

1991   An Taoiseach Charles Haughey T.D. officially opened Phase II on 24th February and also inaugurated a new Access Control Security System. British Airways dropped all routes from UK to Cork, Dublin and Shannon.

1992   Bewleys took over Airport catering in January; Two light aircraft from Iona Flying School collided over Bandon 26th February – one crashed and both occupants were killed; King Karl Gustav of Sweden inspected guard of honour at airport on 9th April; Phase III of Terminal Expansion and Development Pan completed and was officially opened by Maire Geoghan Quinn T.D. Minister for Tourism and Transport 23rd July.

1993   Servisair began operations in Cork in March.

1994   Phase IV of the Development Plan officially opened by Brian   Cowan T.D. Minister for Transport, Energy and Communications on 26th October.

1995   New Freight Terminal and Freight Ramp opened by Hugh Coveney T.D. Minister of State in November.

1996   Bond Helicopters (Ireland) Ltd awarded long term contract by Marathon Petroleum to provide a helicopter service to their two  Kinsale platform from Cork Airport.

1998    In March, Barry Roche Airport General Manager retired and was replaced by Joe O'Connor; Two new freight buildings completed in May. Further extensions to both main and freight ramps. Construction of Airport Business Park began in October.

1999    Covering of asphalt overlay and other necessary work completed on main runway 17/35 in May; Duty Free Sales within the EU ended 30th June; Passenger traffic reached over 1.5 million at end of the year.

2000    Catering franchise split in summer of '00 – Kylemore obtained bar and airport franchise and Alpha the flight catering; Cork Airport opened a new look Travel Value Shop in November.

2001    Cork Airport Great Southern Hotel opened for business 20th March -.official opening on 31st May by Mary O'Rourke, T.D., Minister for Public Enterprise. Extension of northern ramp and taxiway began.

# PASSENGER INFORMATION

| | | |
|---|---|---|
| Airport | Aer Rianta | 021-4313131 |
| Management | Direct Dial | 329-Extn. |
| Duty Office   Fax | | 021-4313442 |
| Duty Free Shop | | 021-4329645 |
| Emergency Night | Number | 021-4313288 |
| Aer Arann | Reservations | 01-8141058 |
| | Fax | 01-8145250 |
| Aer Lingus | Flight Information | 021-4327100 |
| Reservations | | 021-4327155 |
| Passenger Baggage | | 021-4327112 |
| Fax | | 021-4327150 |
| Cargo | | 021-4327131 |
| Aer Wales | Reservations | 0044-1444-882000 |
| British European | Reservations | 1890-925532 |
| BA City Flyer | Reservations | 1800-626747 |

| Brymon Airways | Reservations | 1800-626747 |
| & Manx Airlines | Flight Information | 021-4327100 |
| Europe | | |
| CHC (Ireland) | Operations | 021-4312128 |
| Helicopters | Fax | 021-4312461 |
| Keenair | Reservations | 021-4642217 |
| Ryanair | Reservations | 01-6097800 |

Servisair

Handling Agents for Ryanair, CityFlyer,

British Regional Airlines, Brymon Airways.

| Flight Information | | 021-4329677 |
| | Fax | 021-4313506 |
| Passenger Baggage | | 021-4313091 |
| Cargo | | 021-4310987 |
| | | 021-4310988 |
| | Fax | 021-4310837 |

# Index